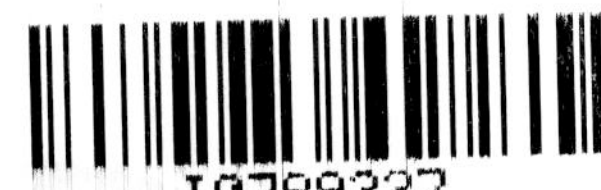

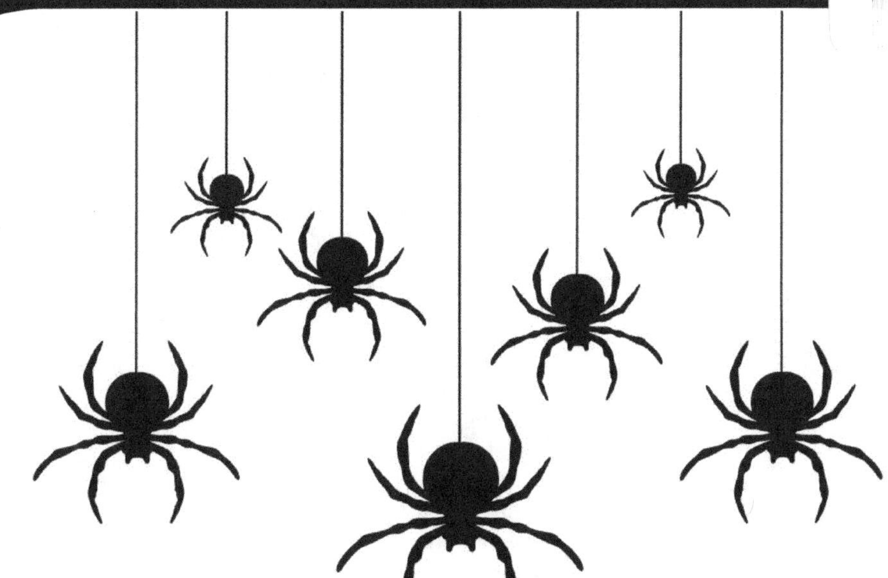

Halloween Coloring Book for Kids

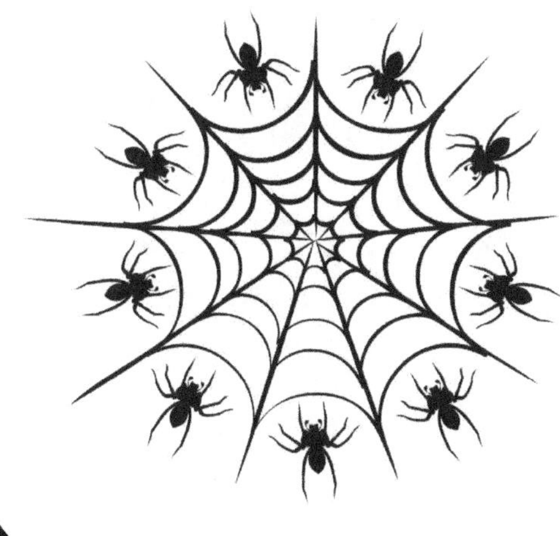

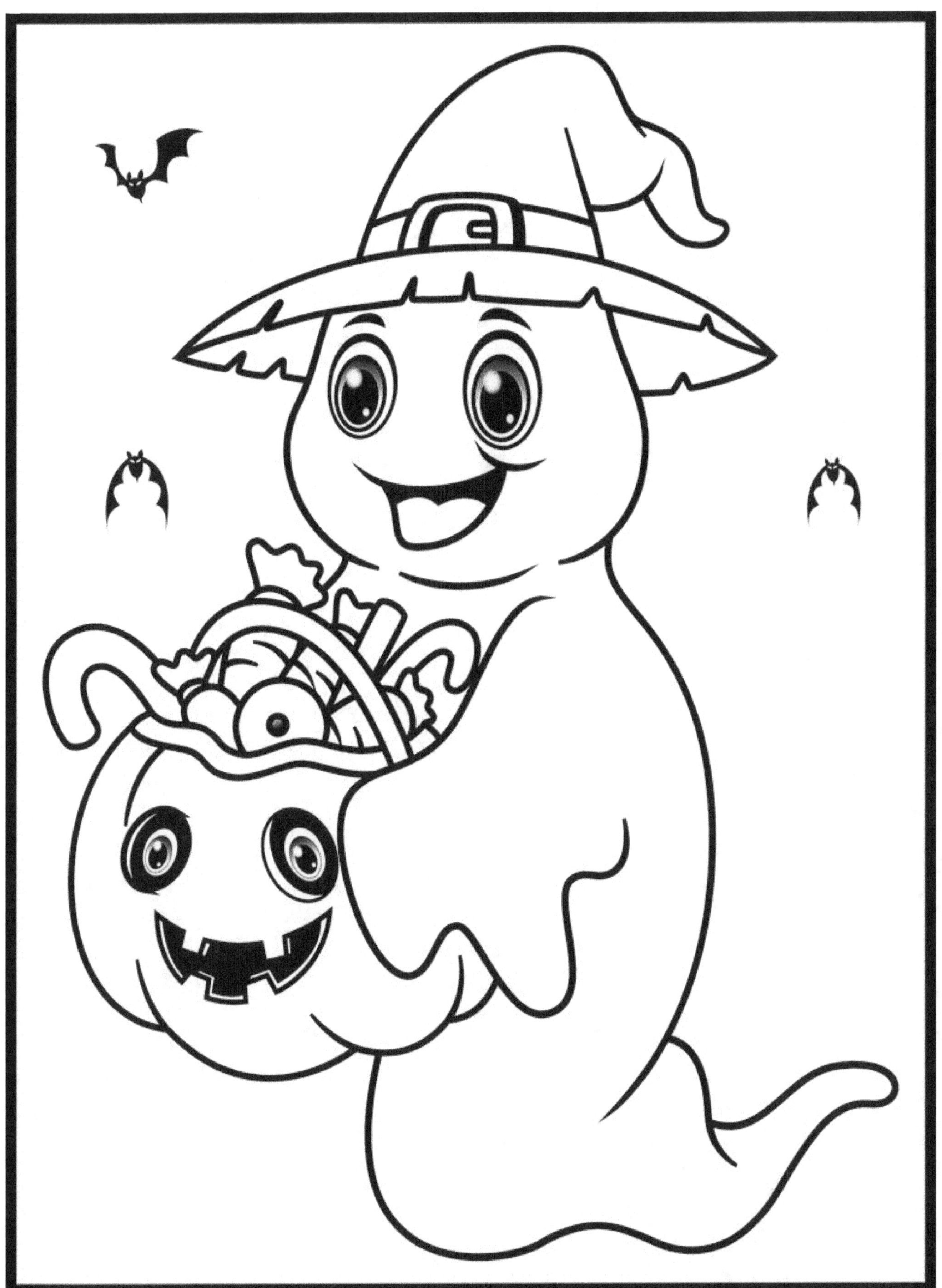

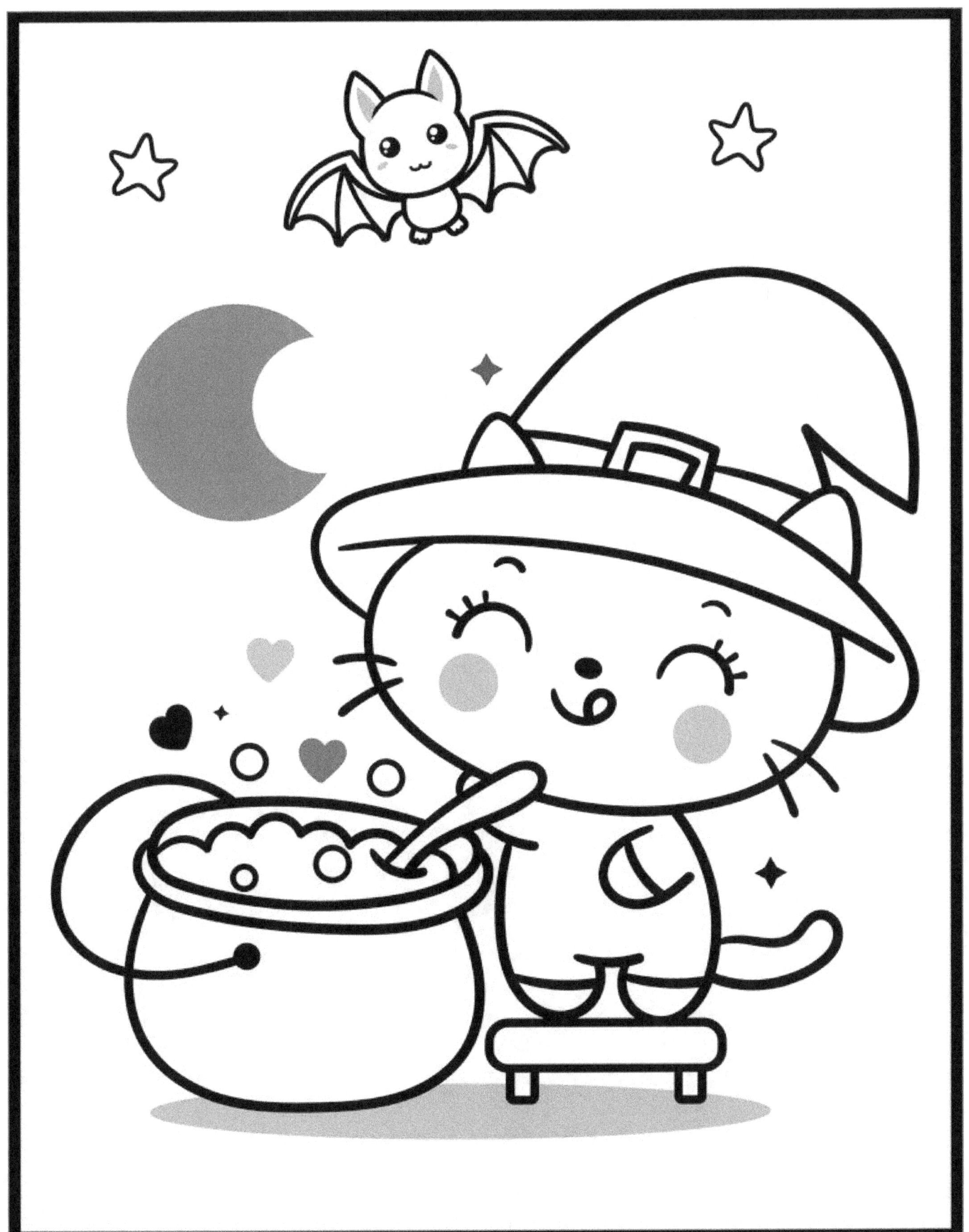

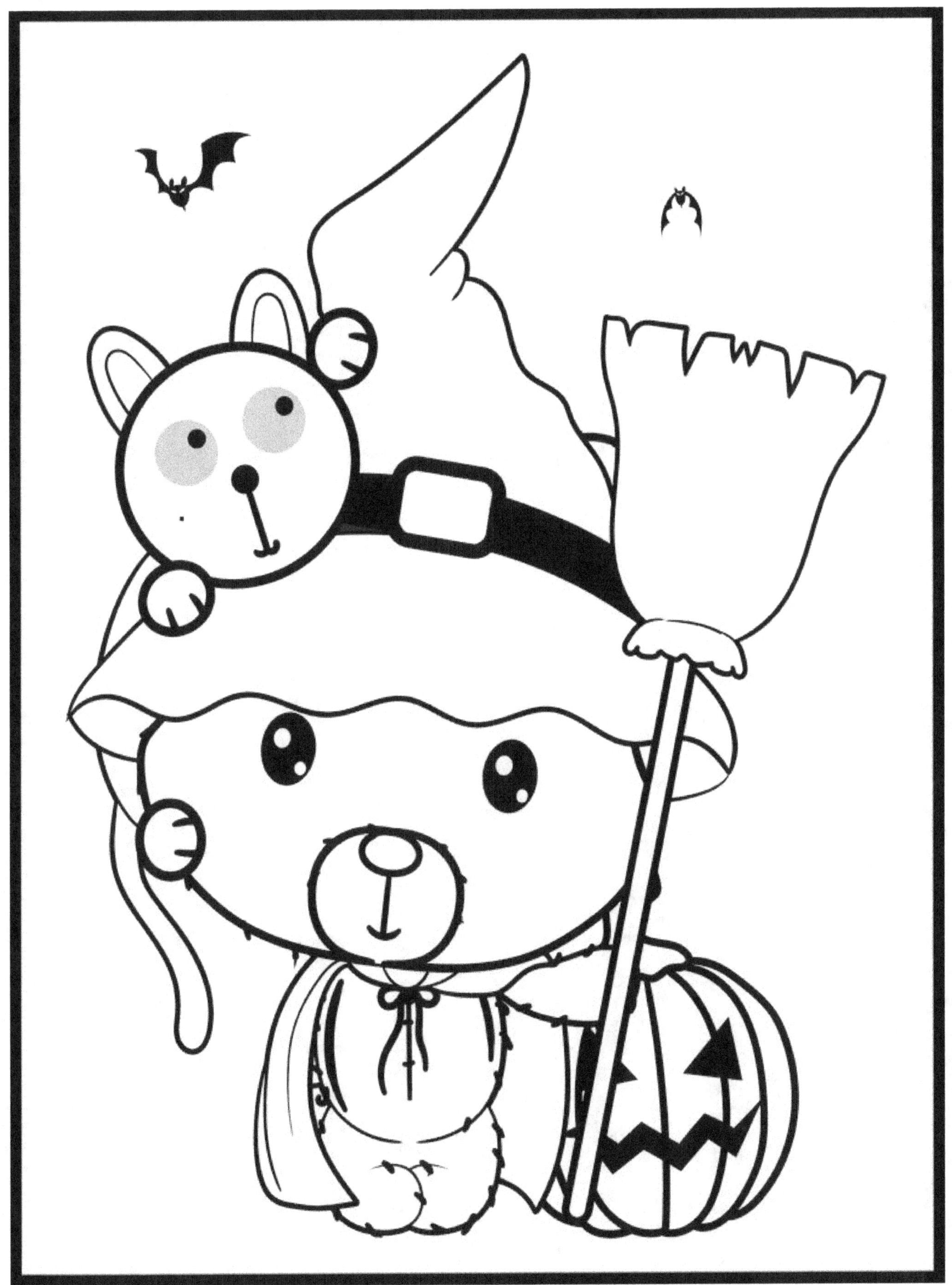

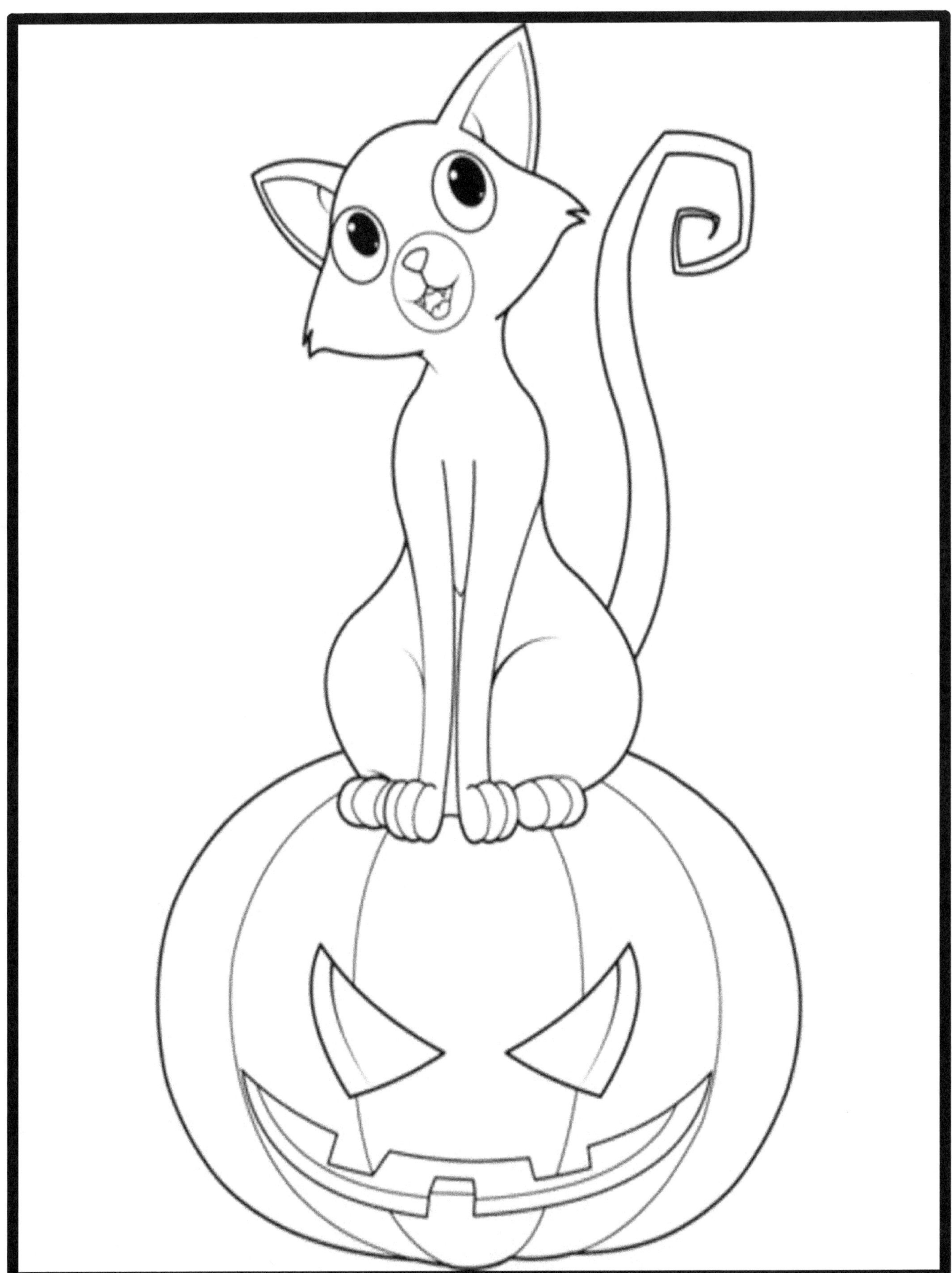

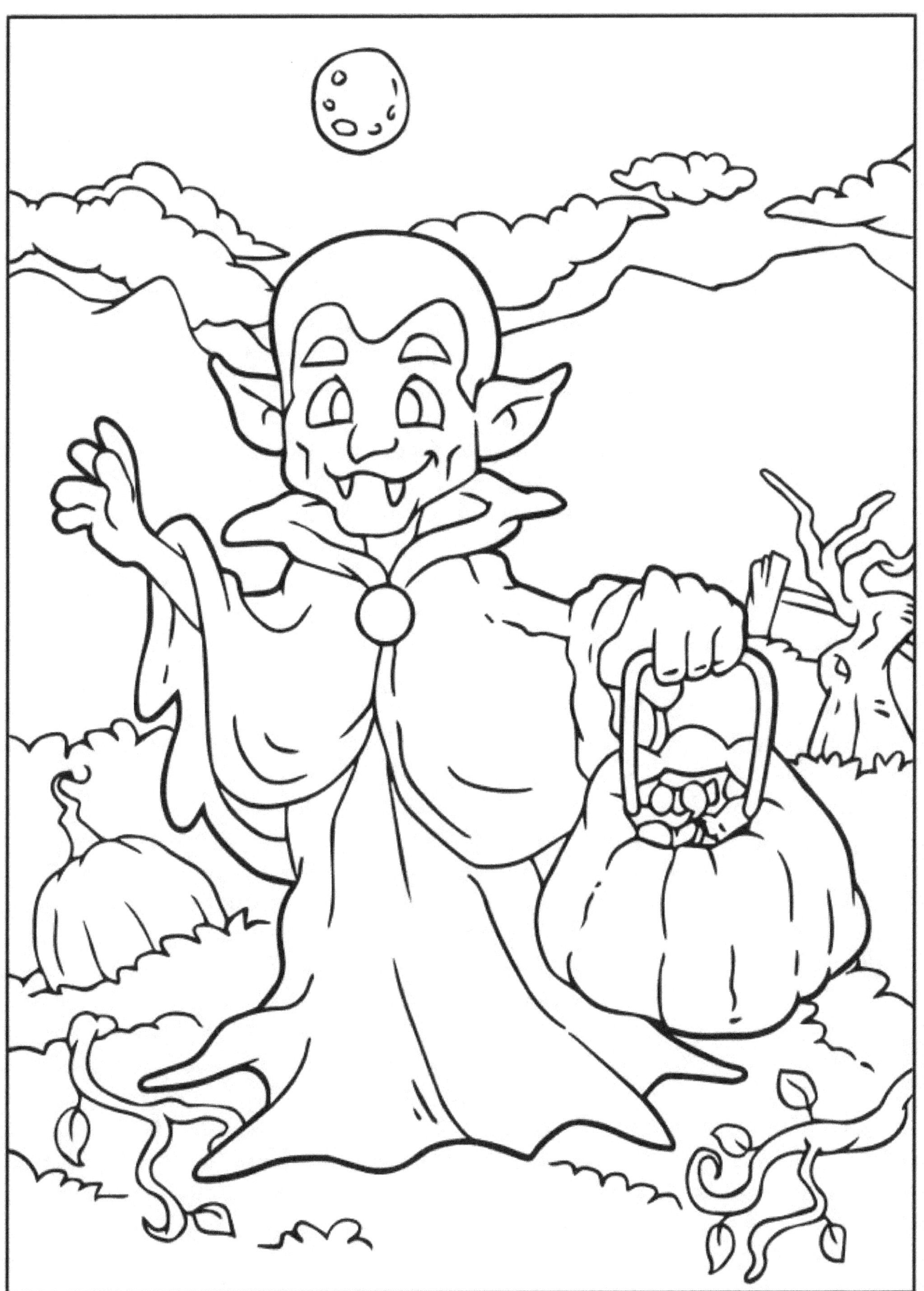

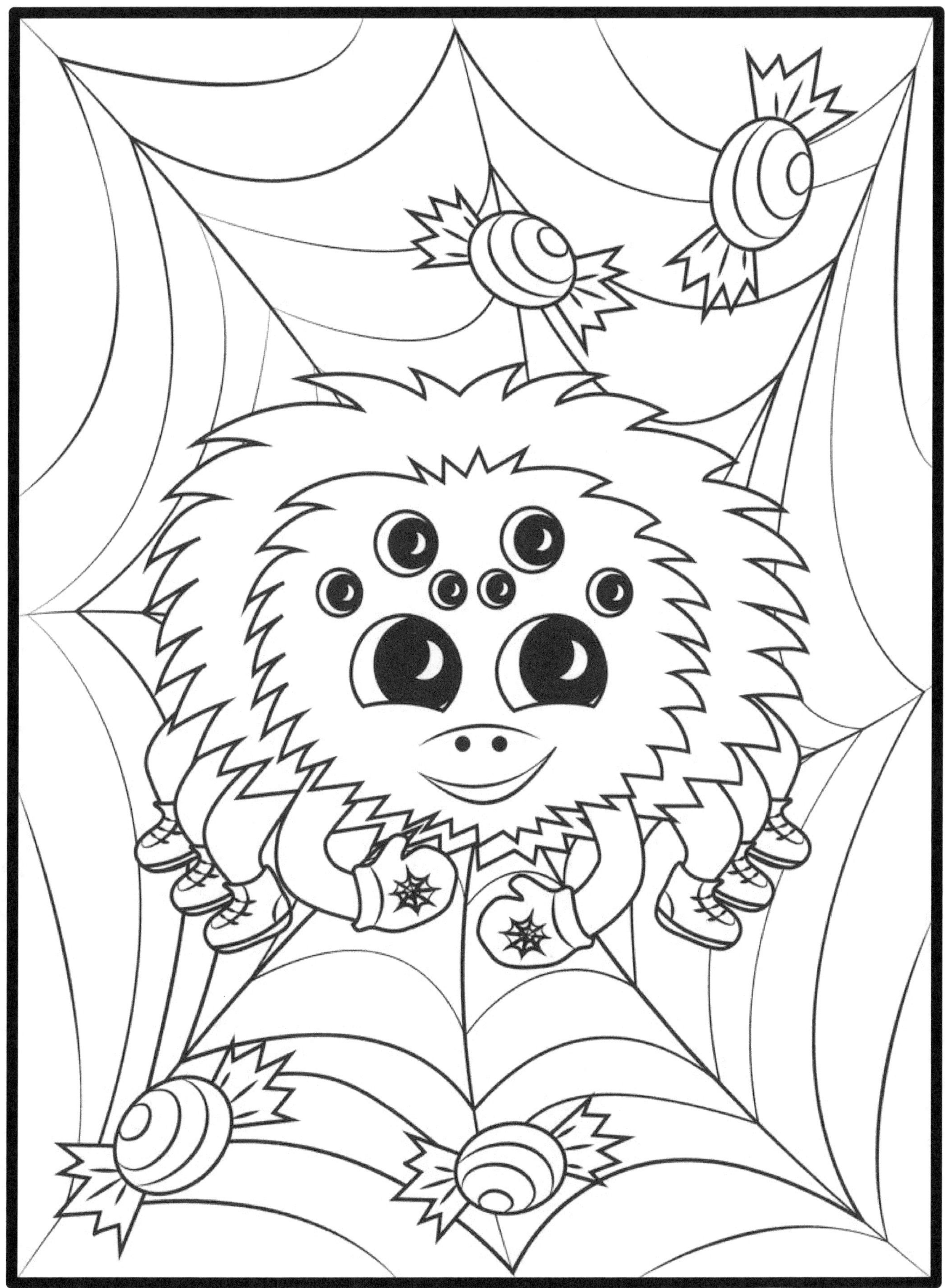

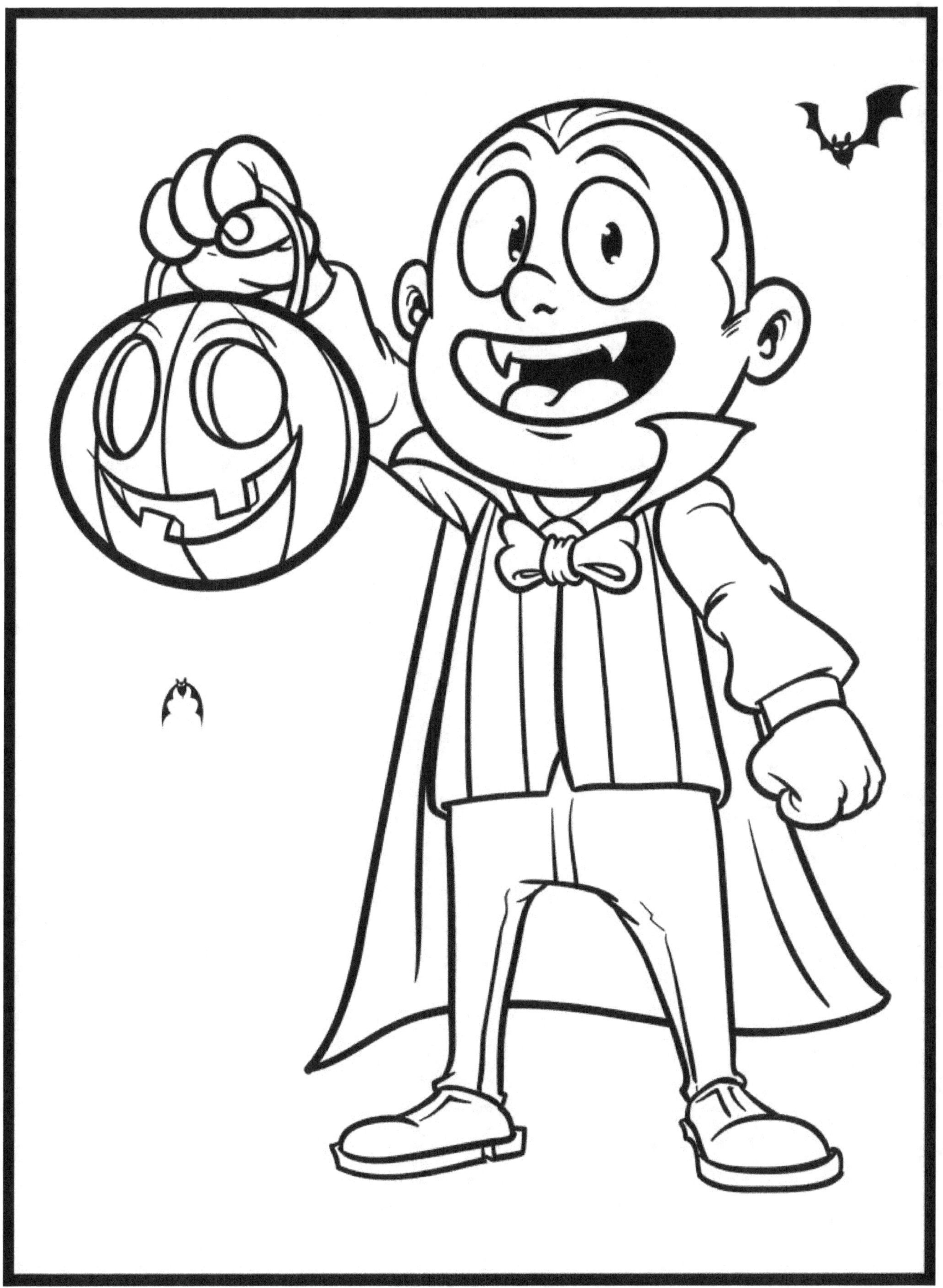

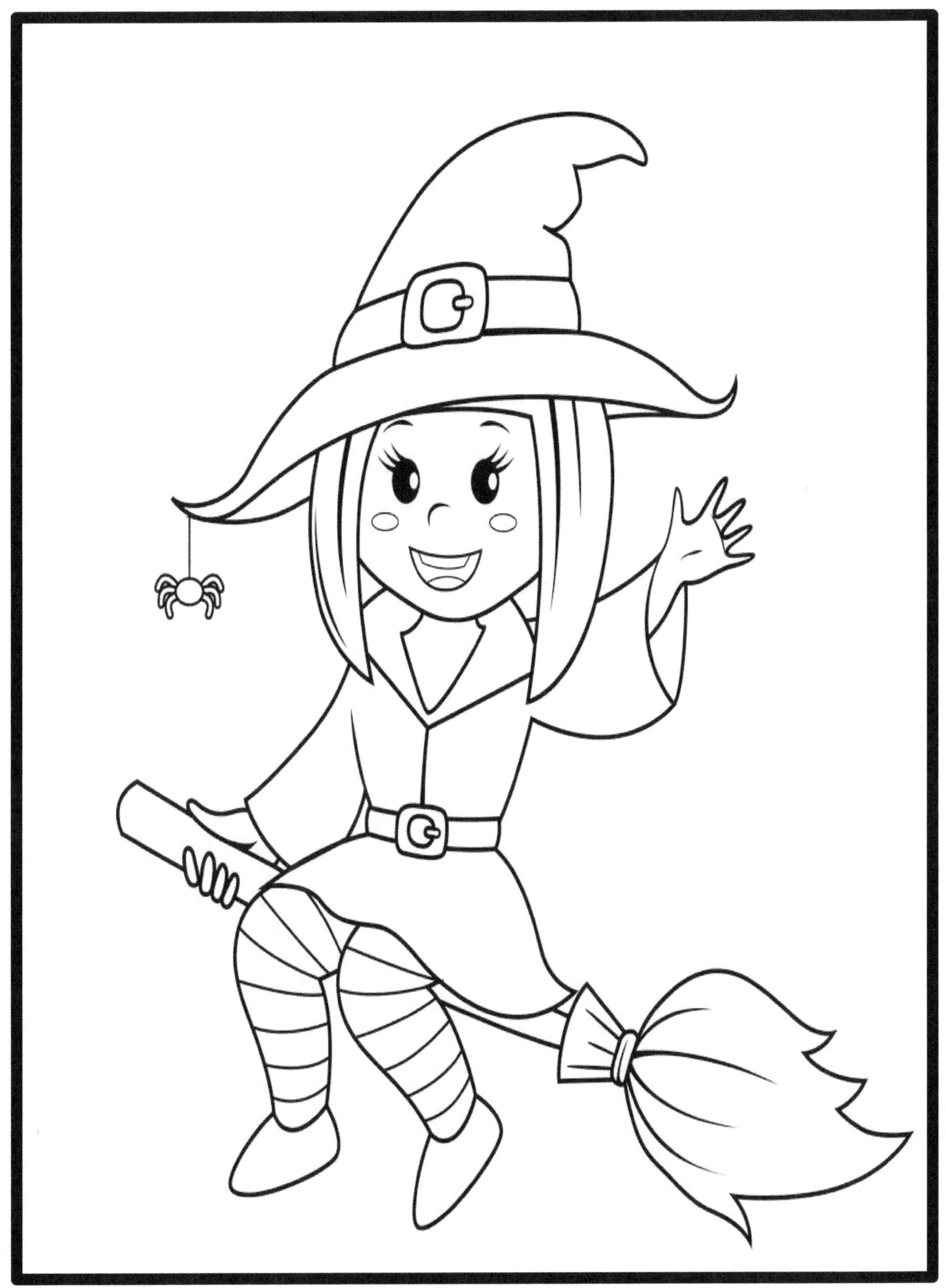

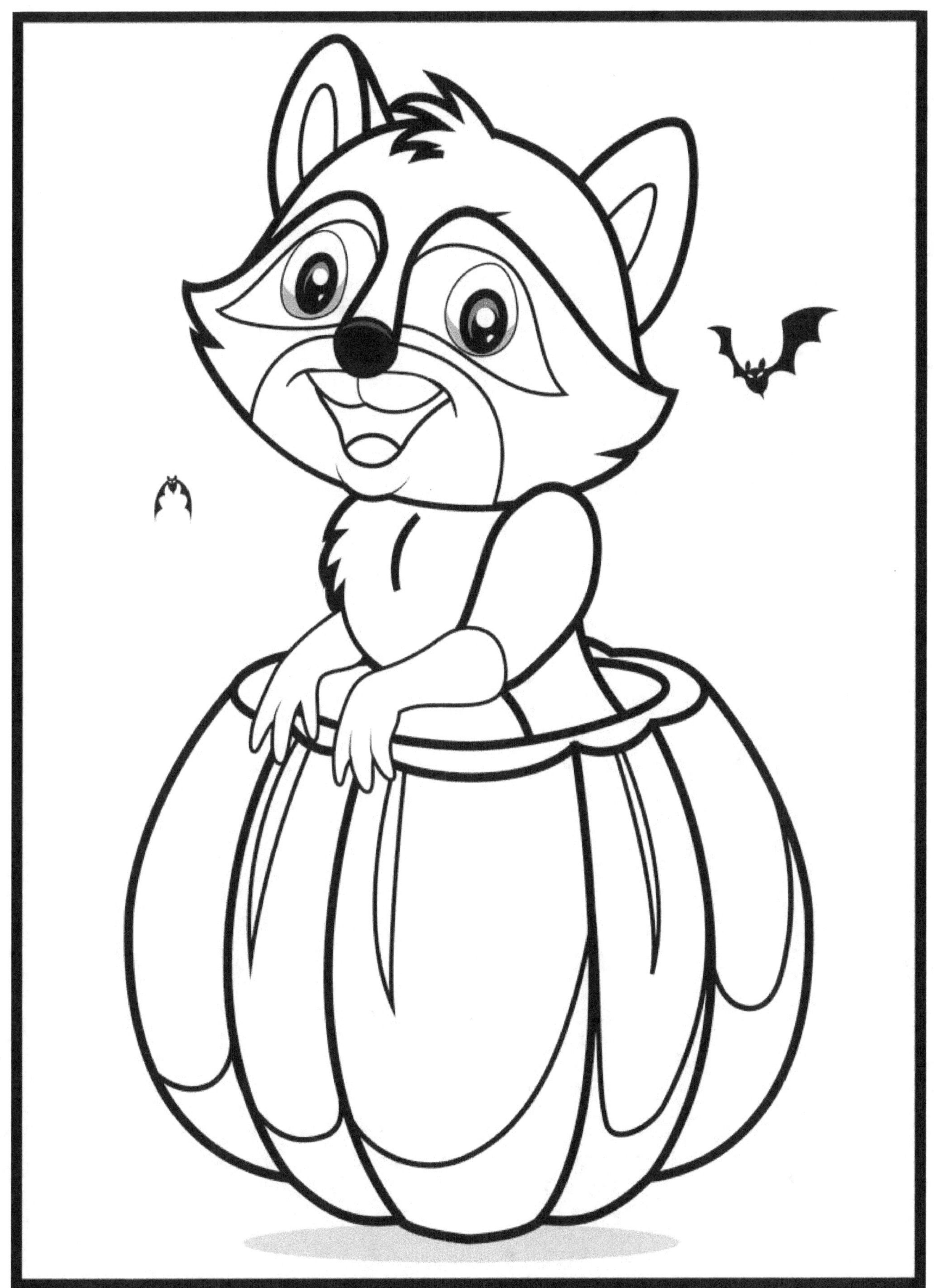

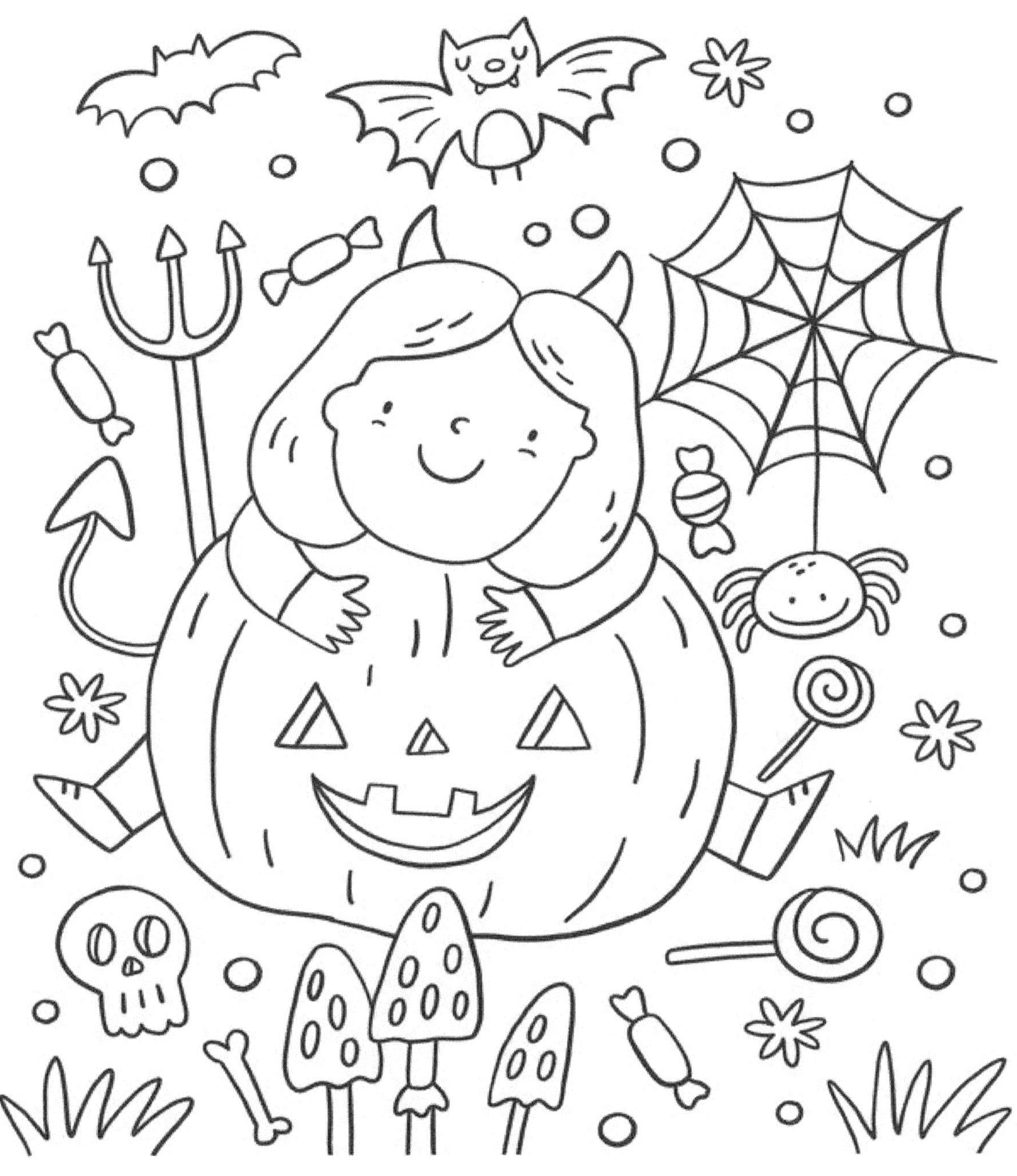

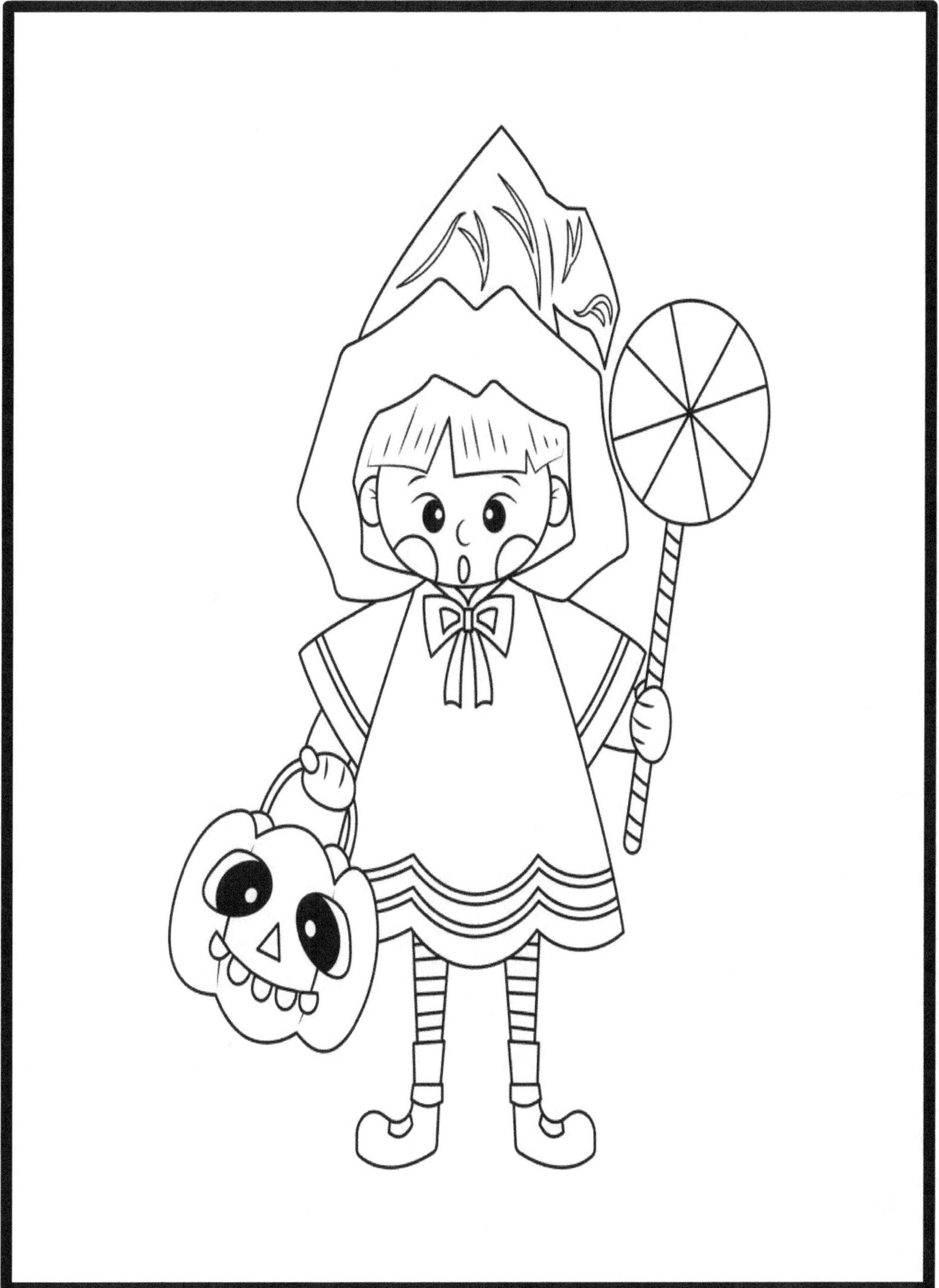

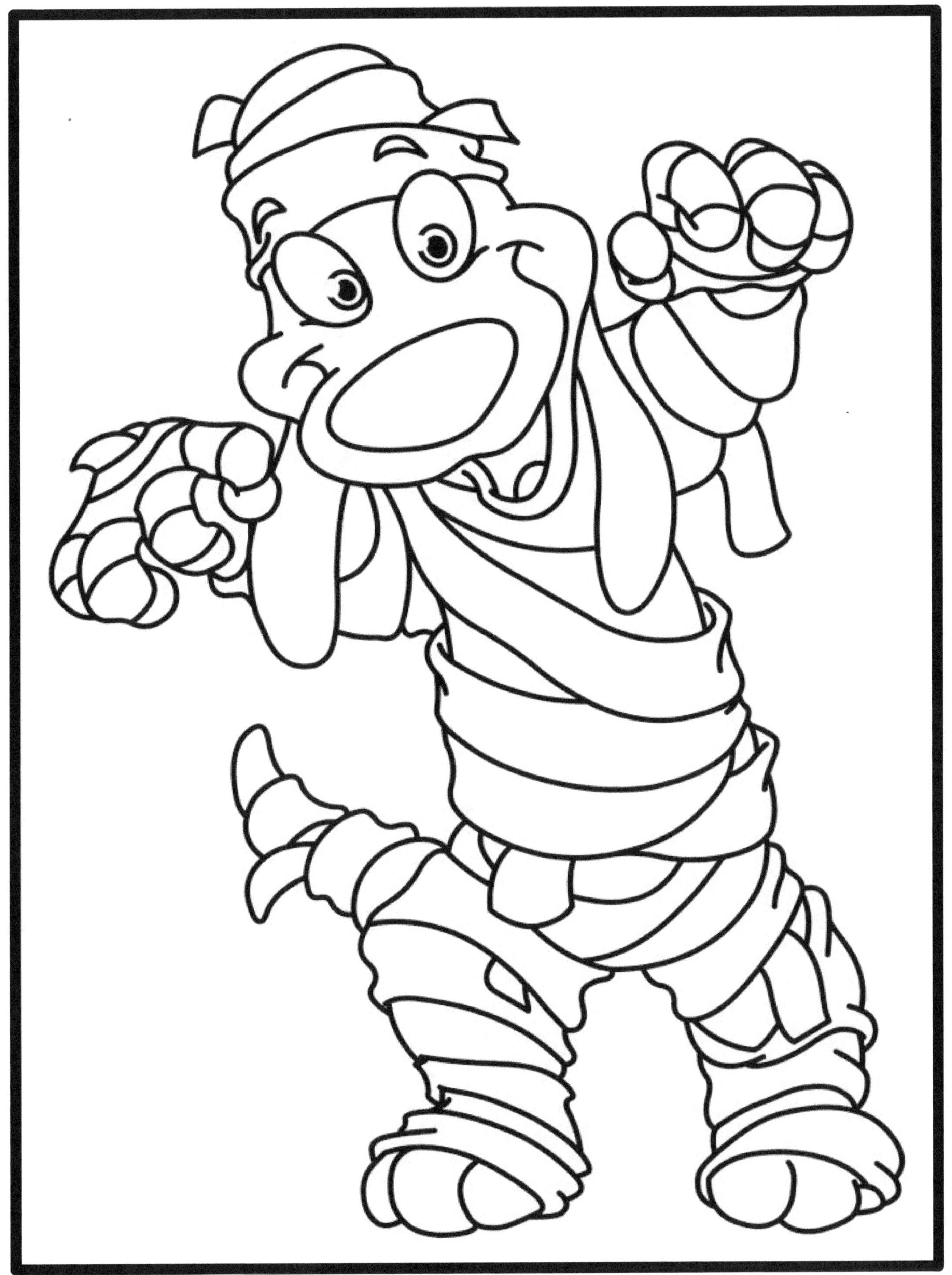

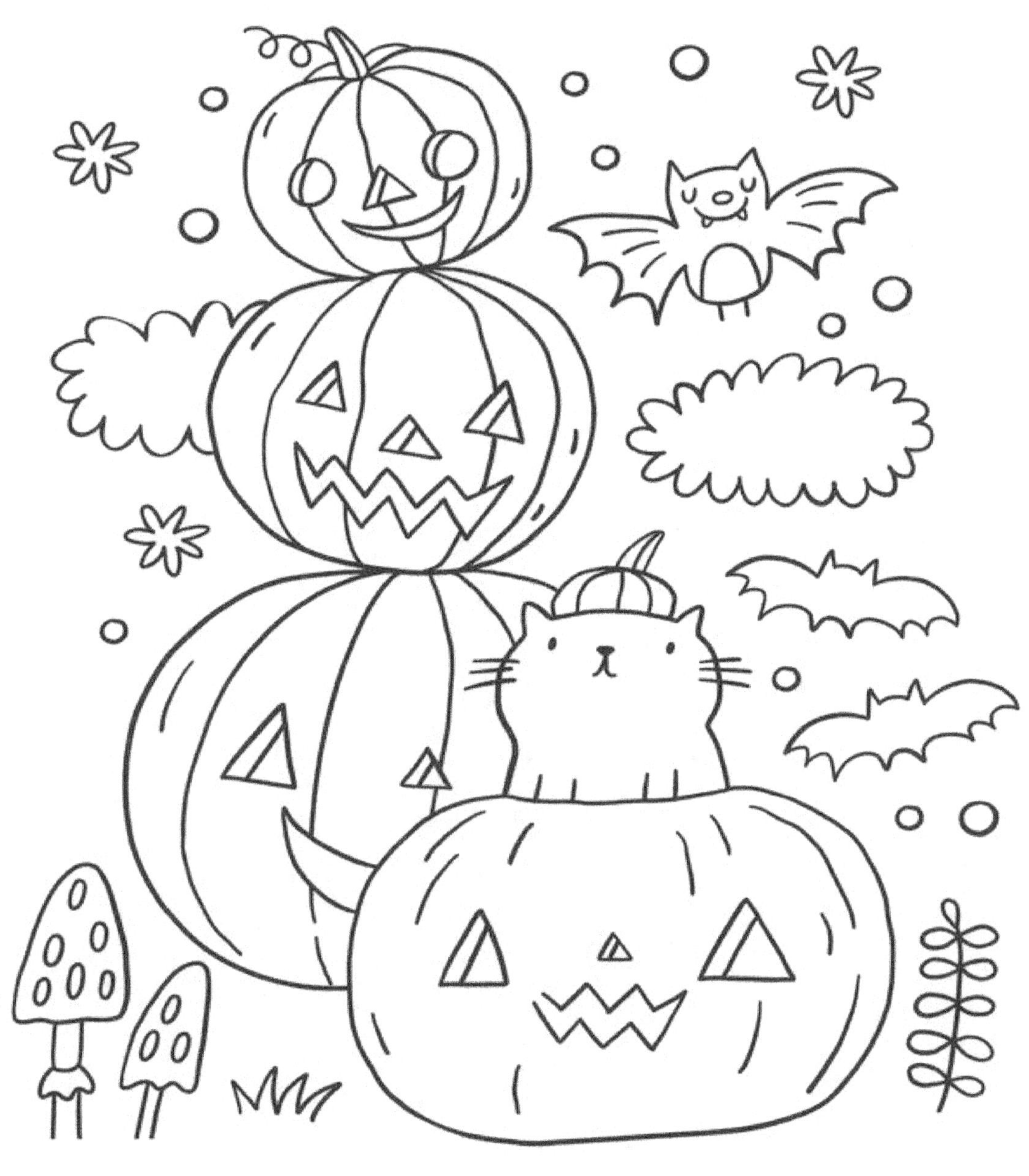

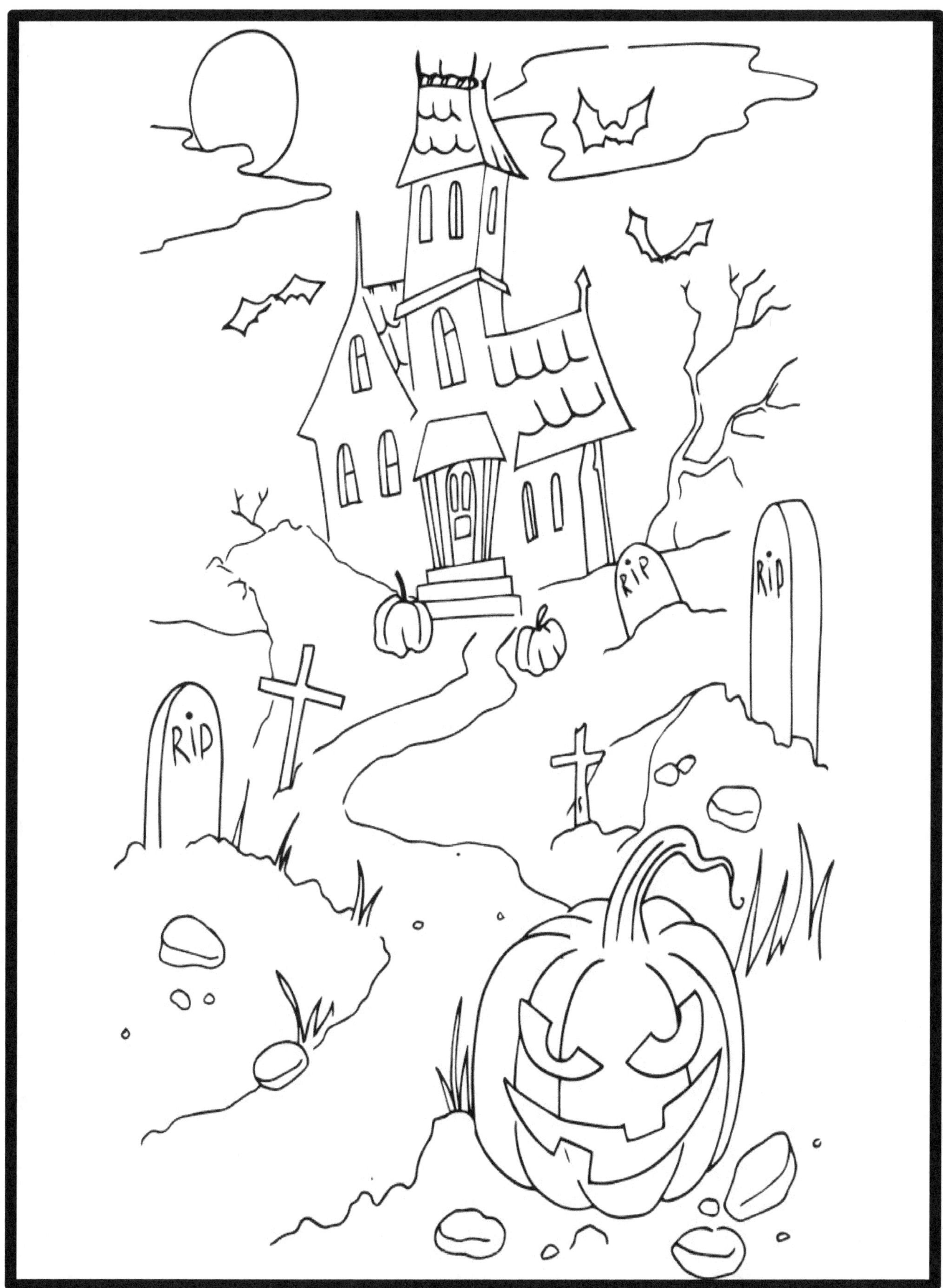

RIP
RIP
RIP

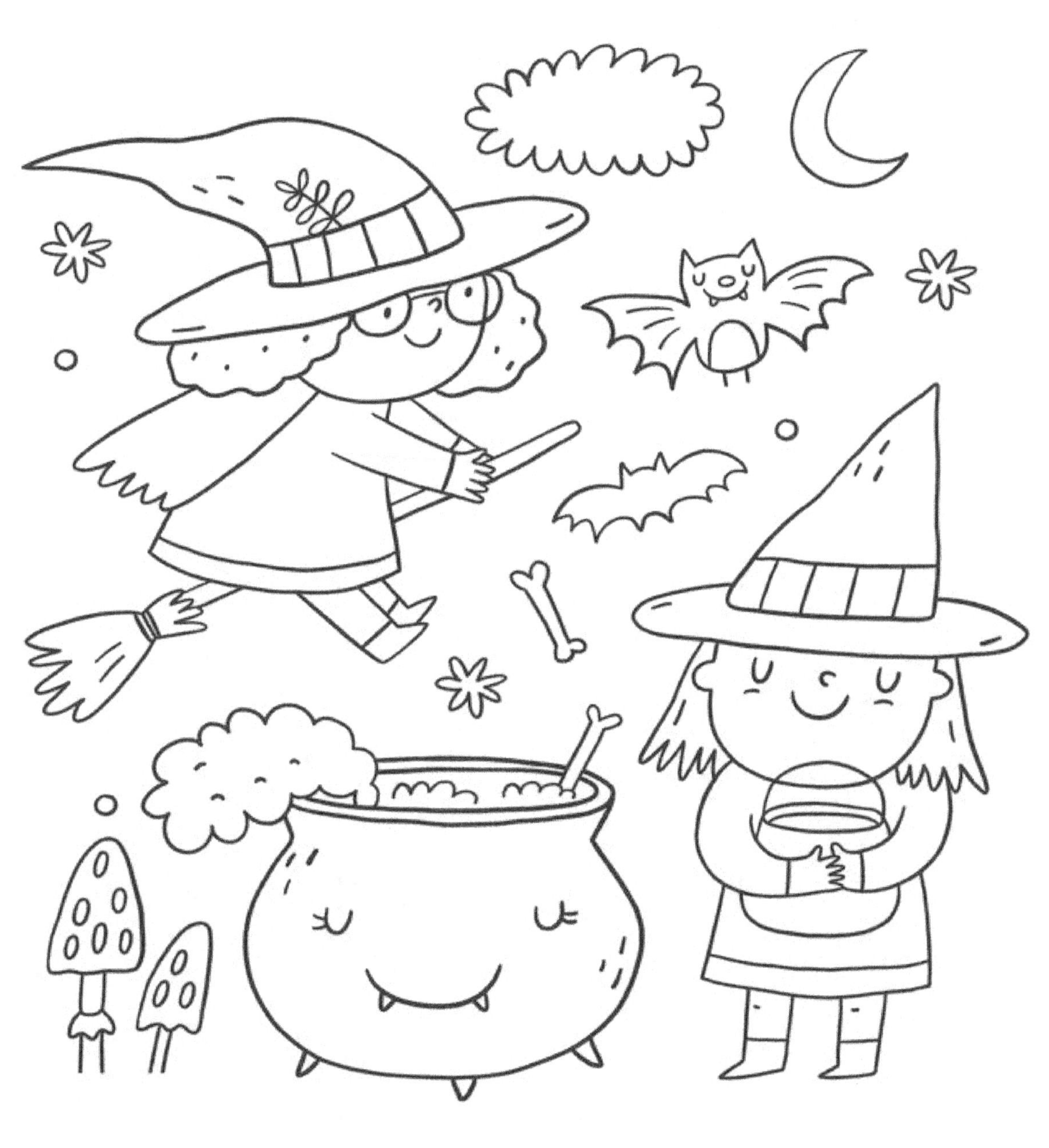

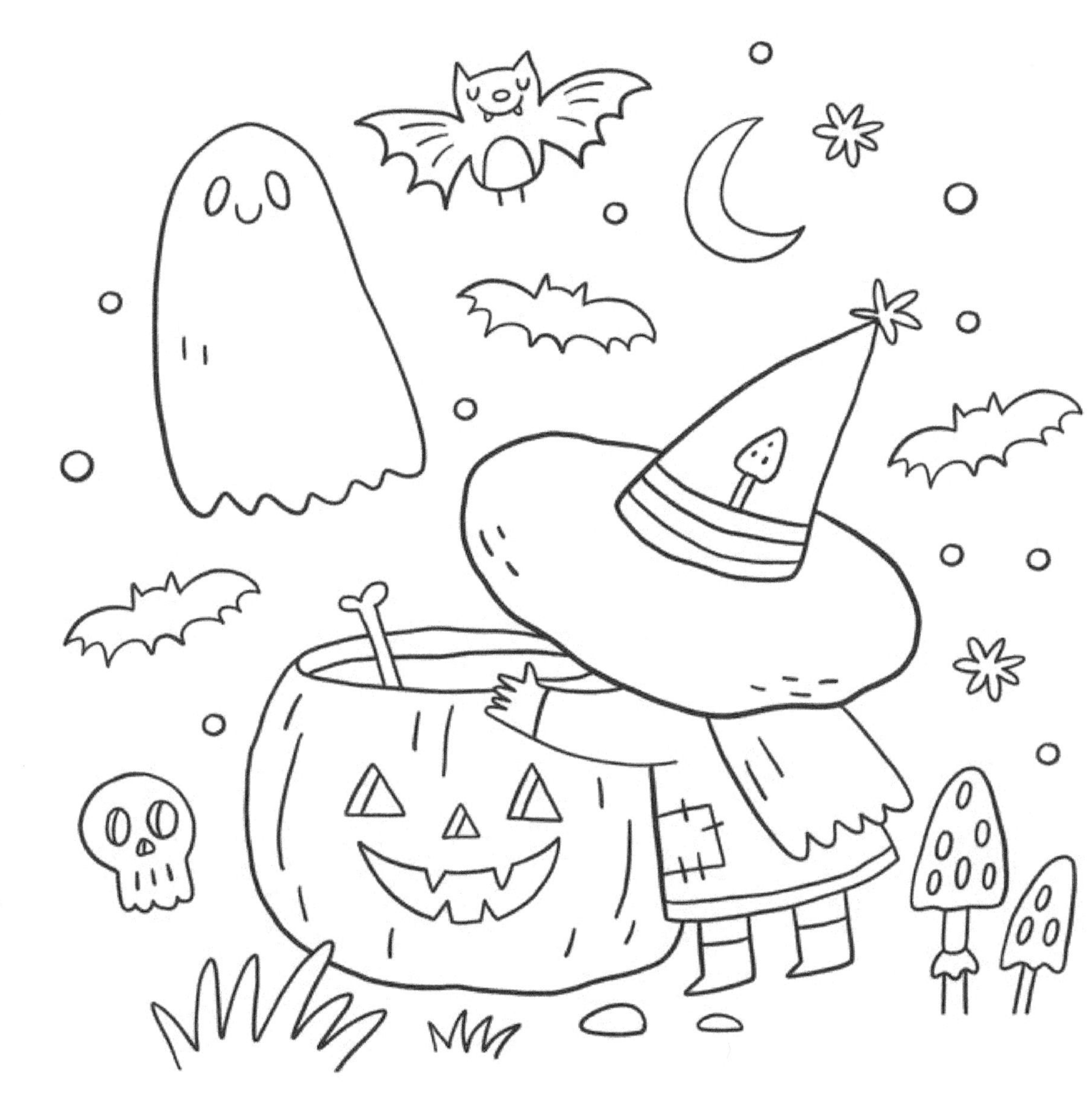

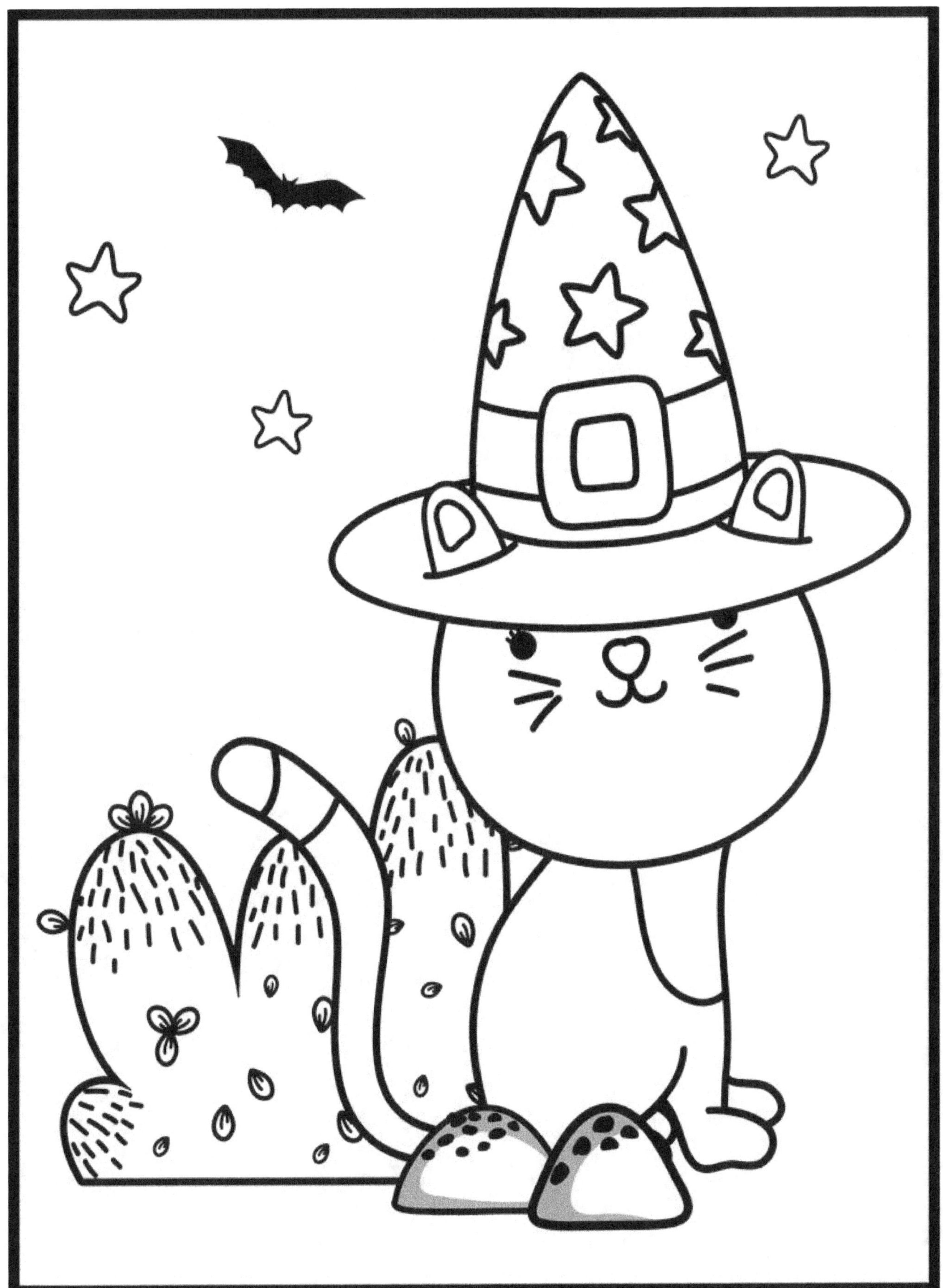

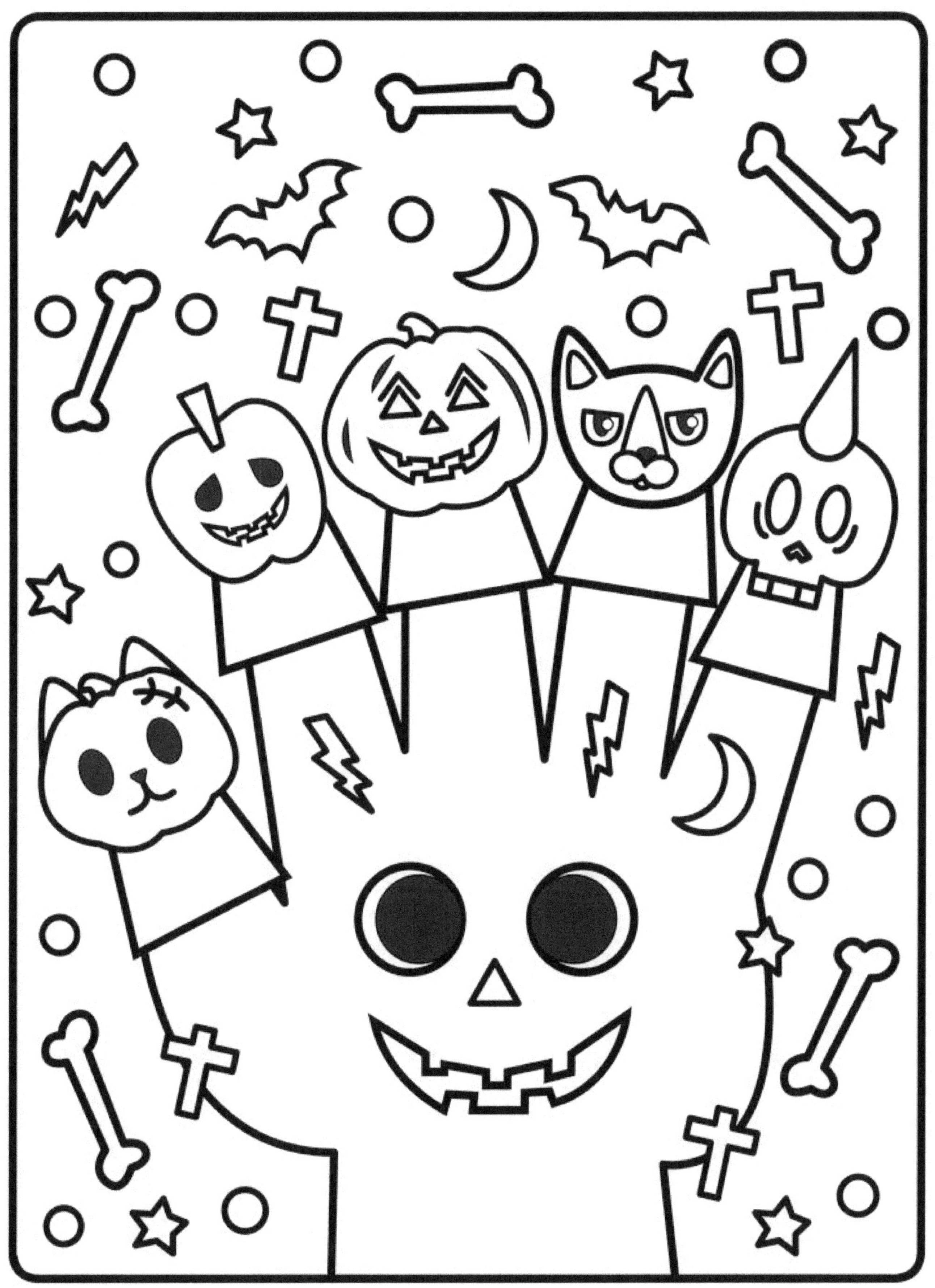

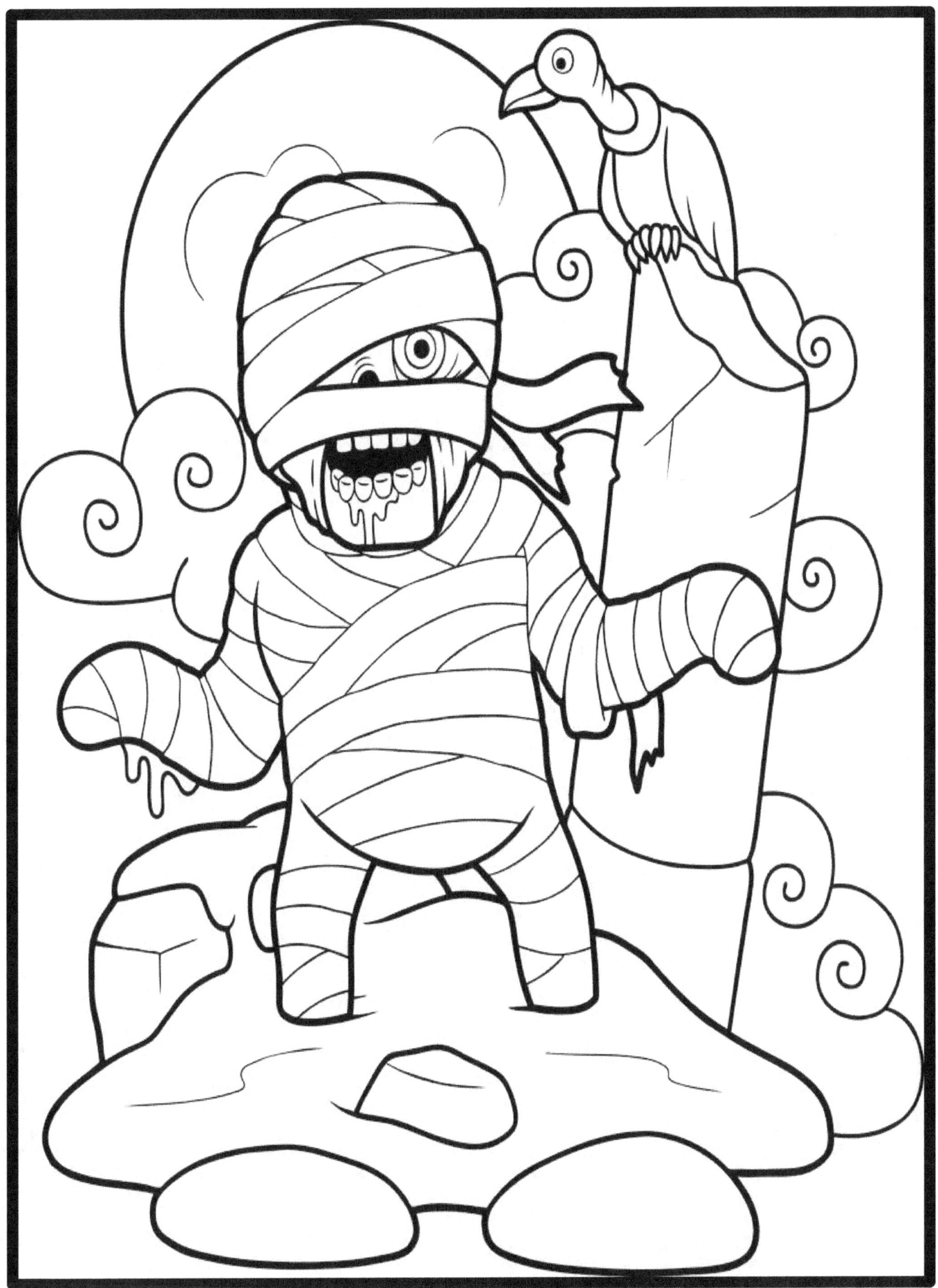

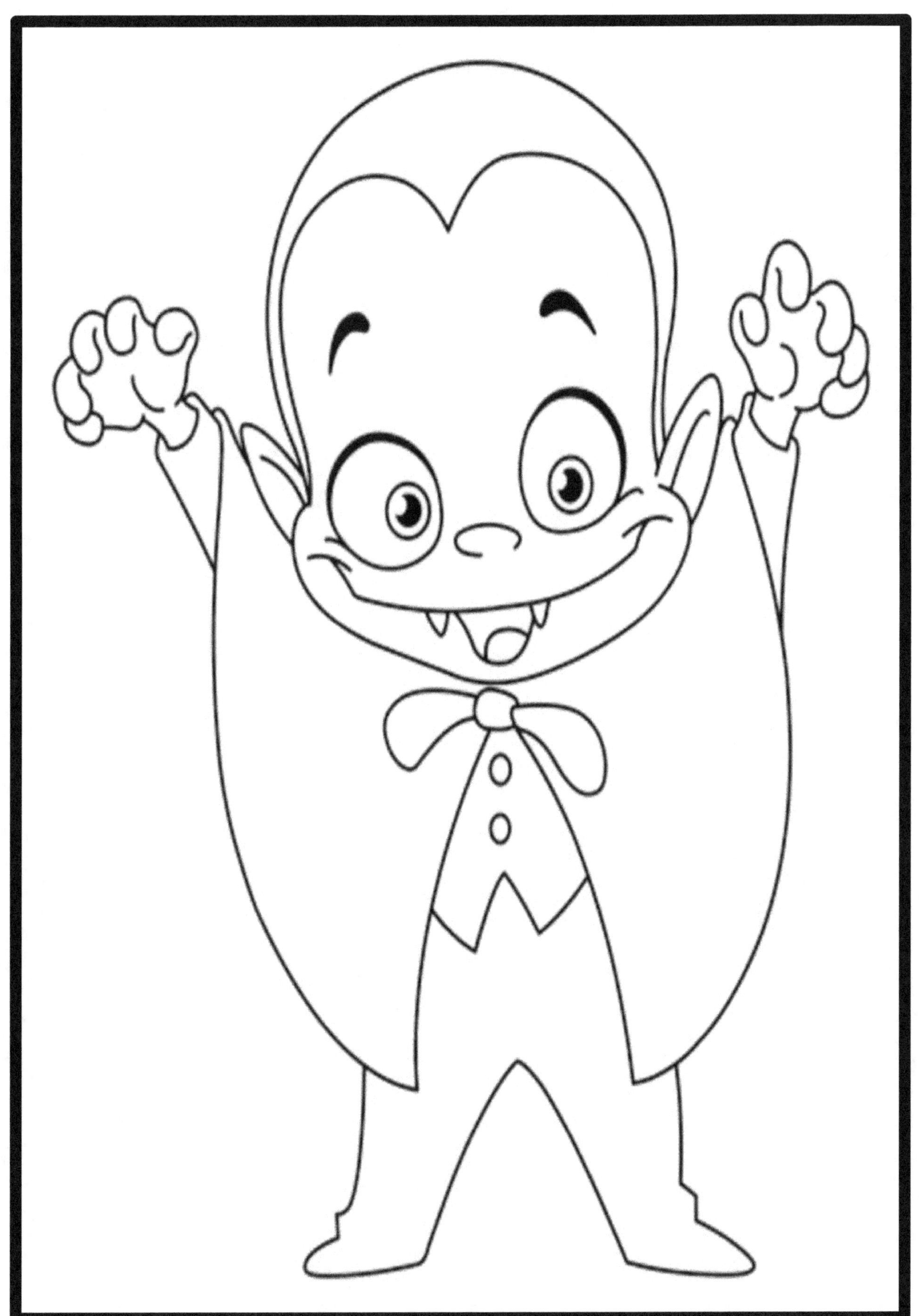

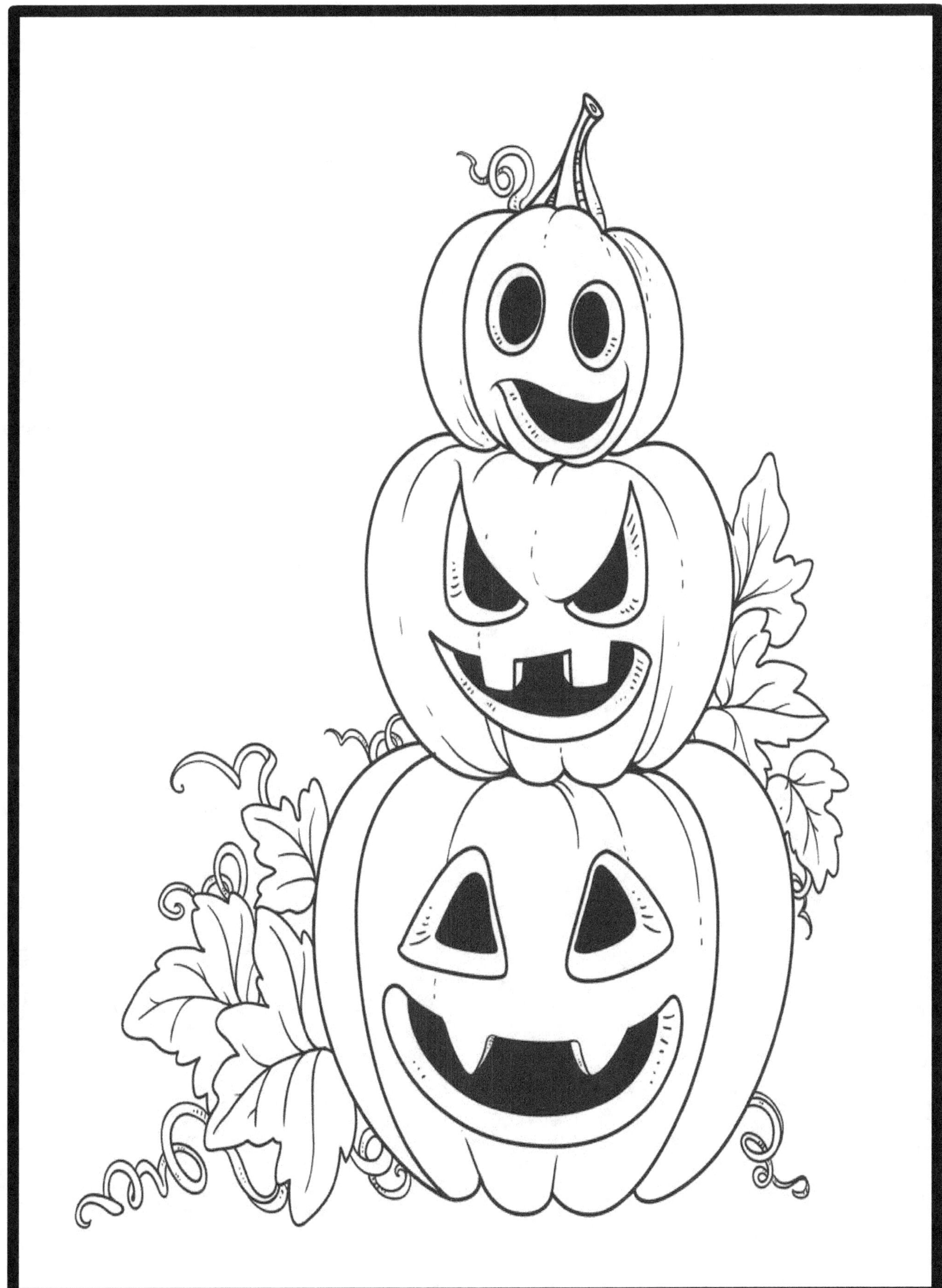

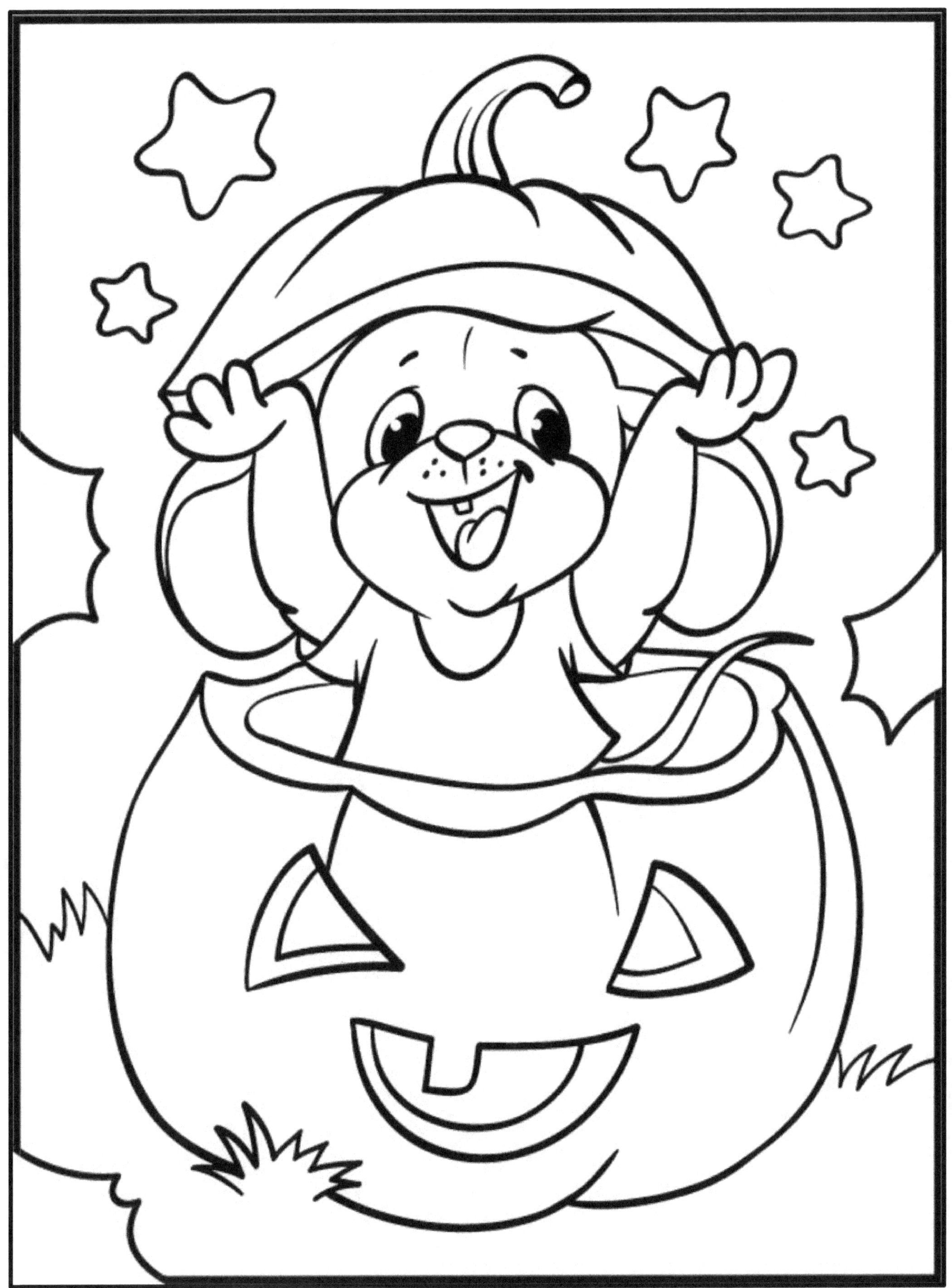

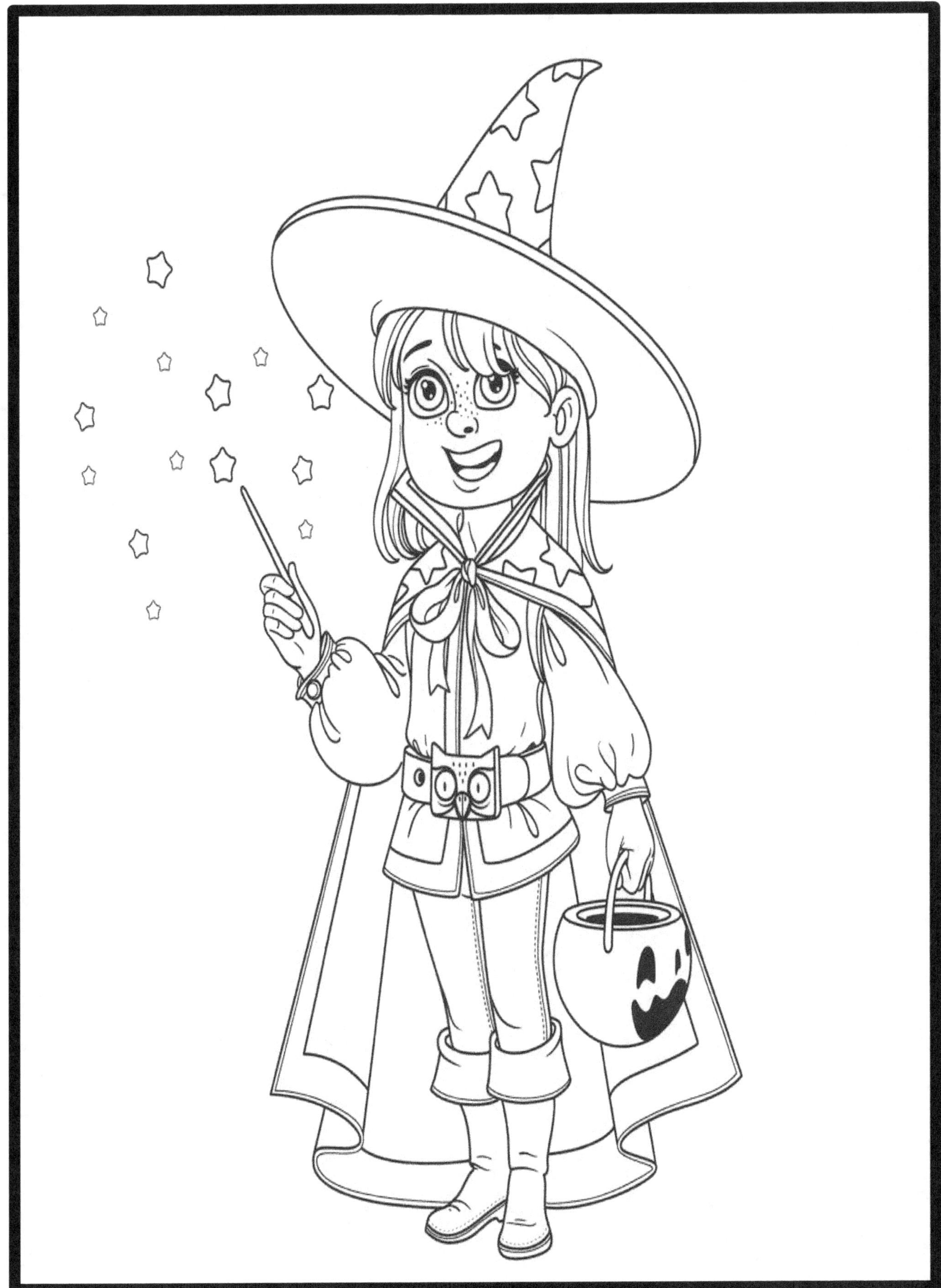

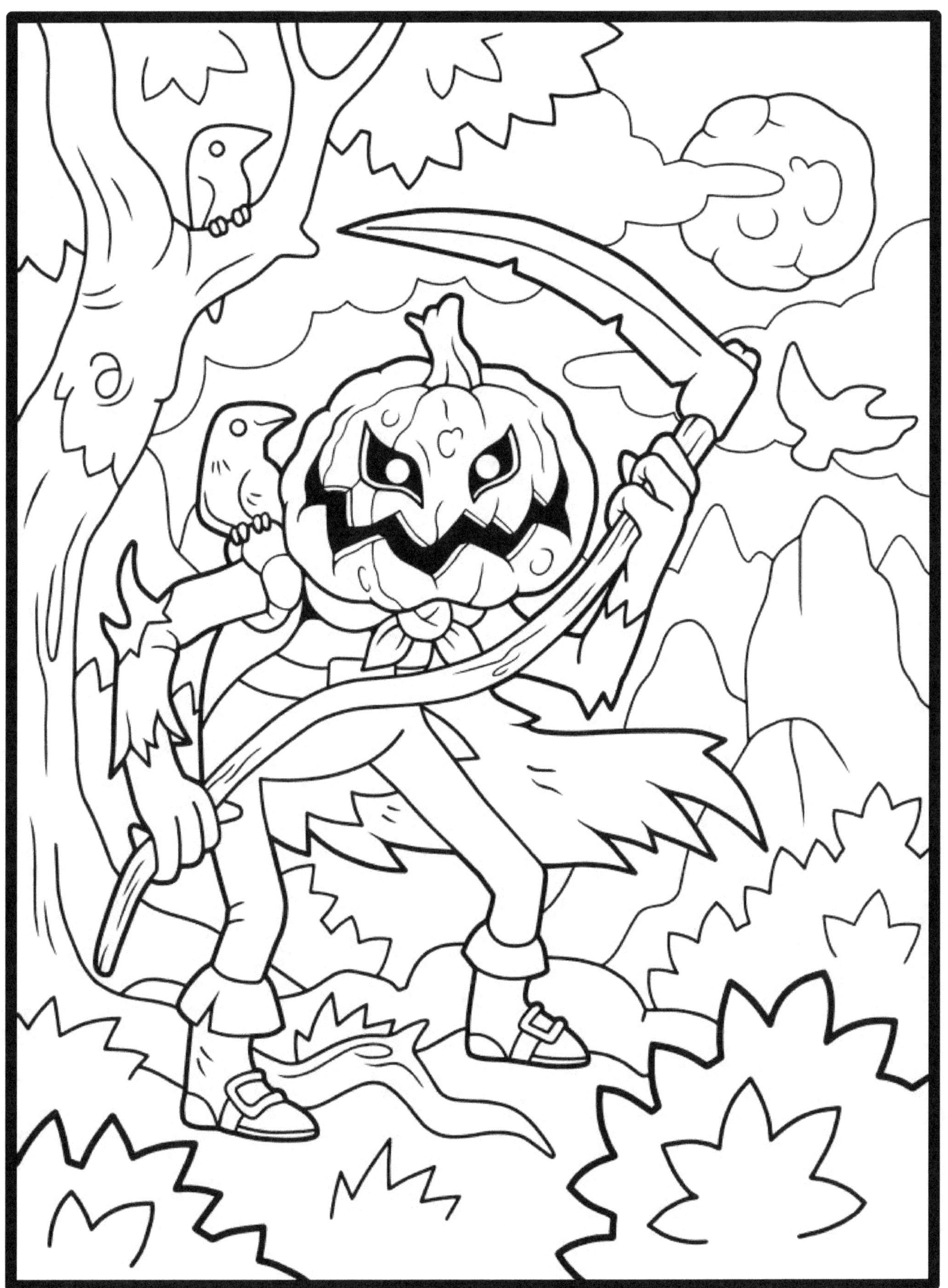

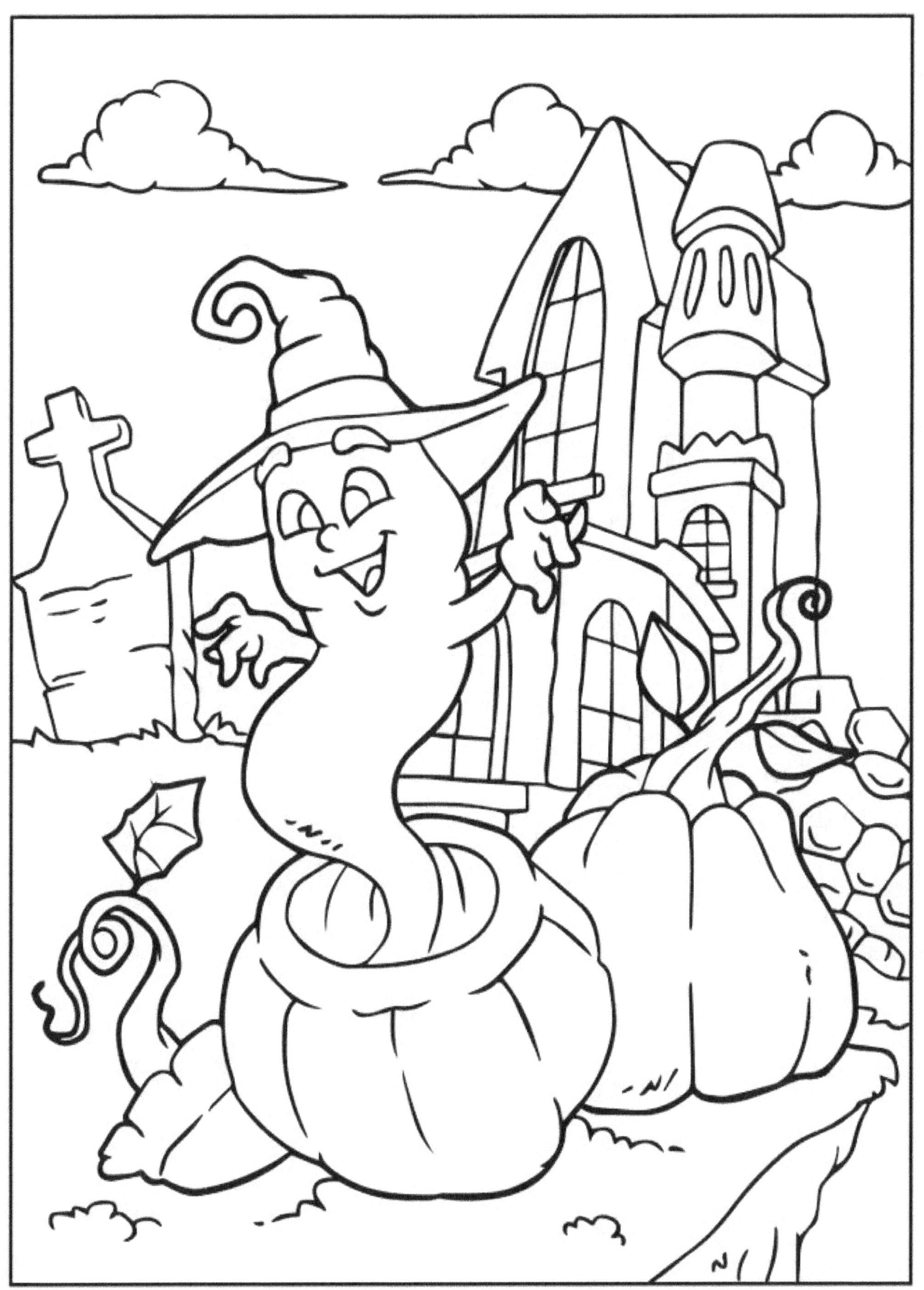

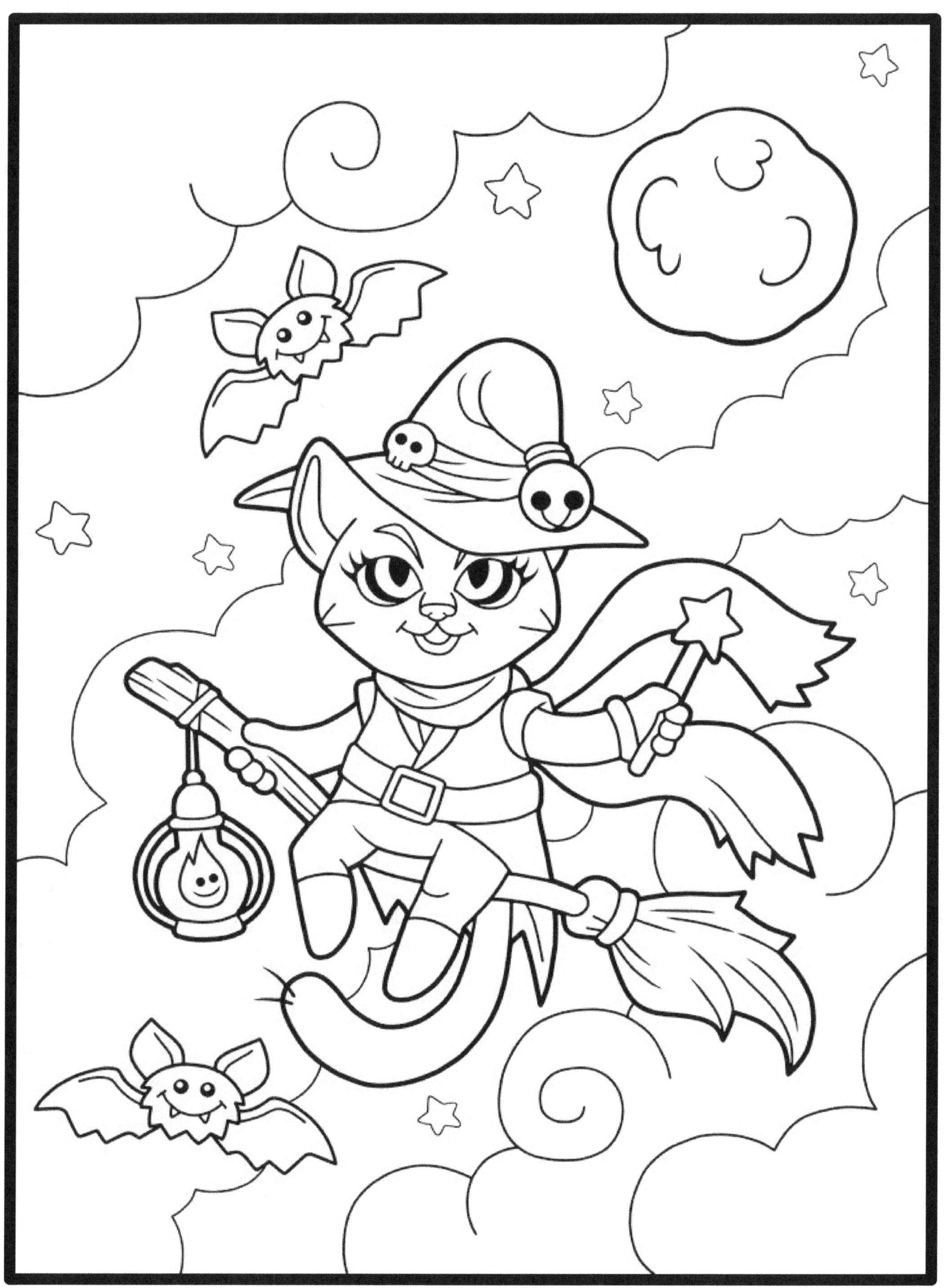

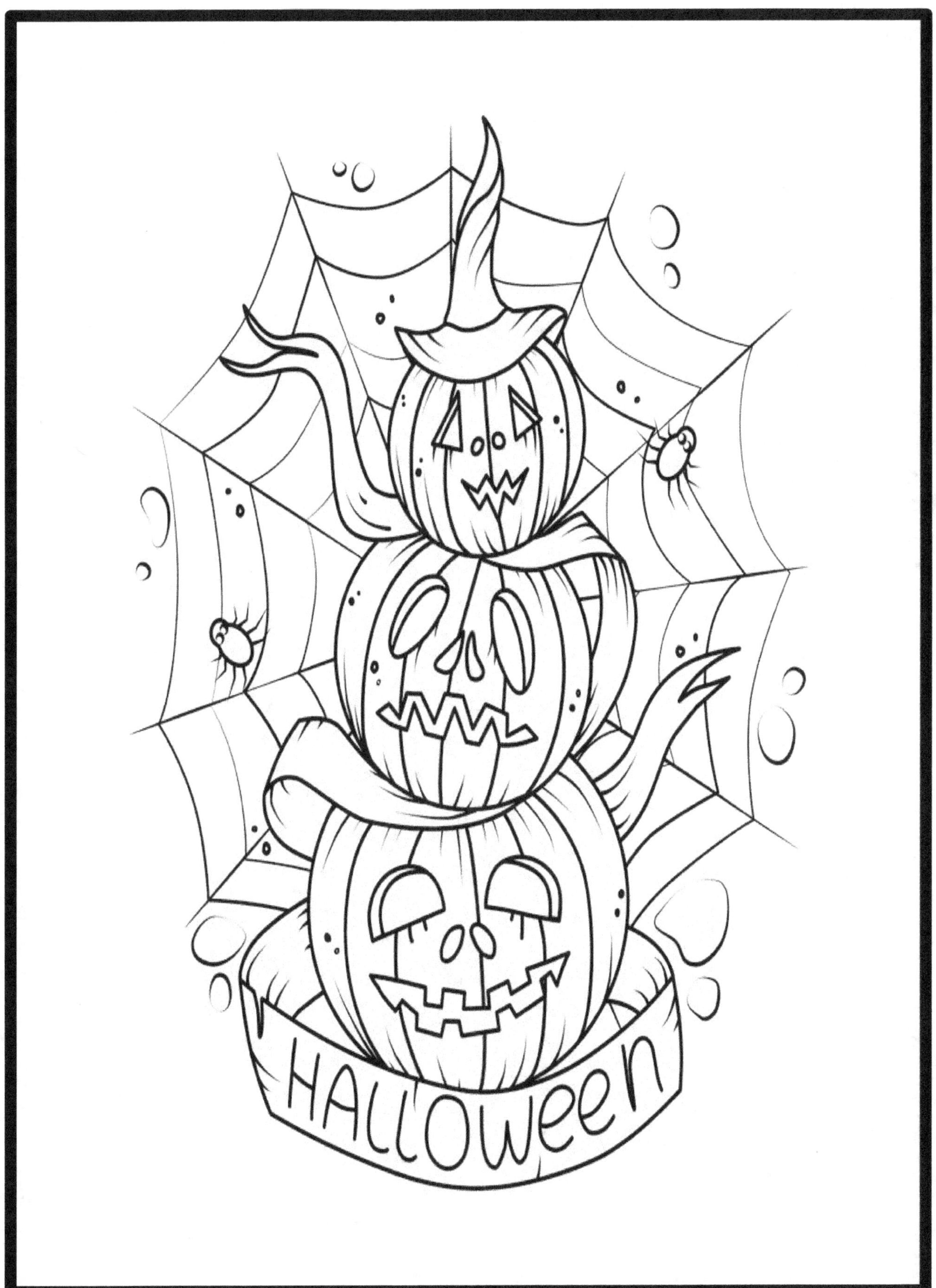

HALLOWEEN

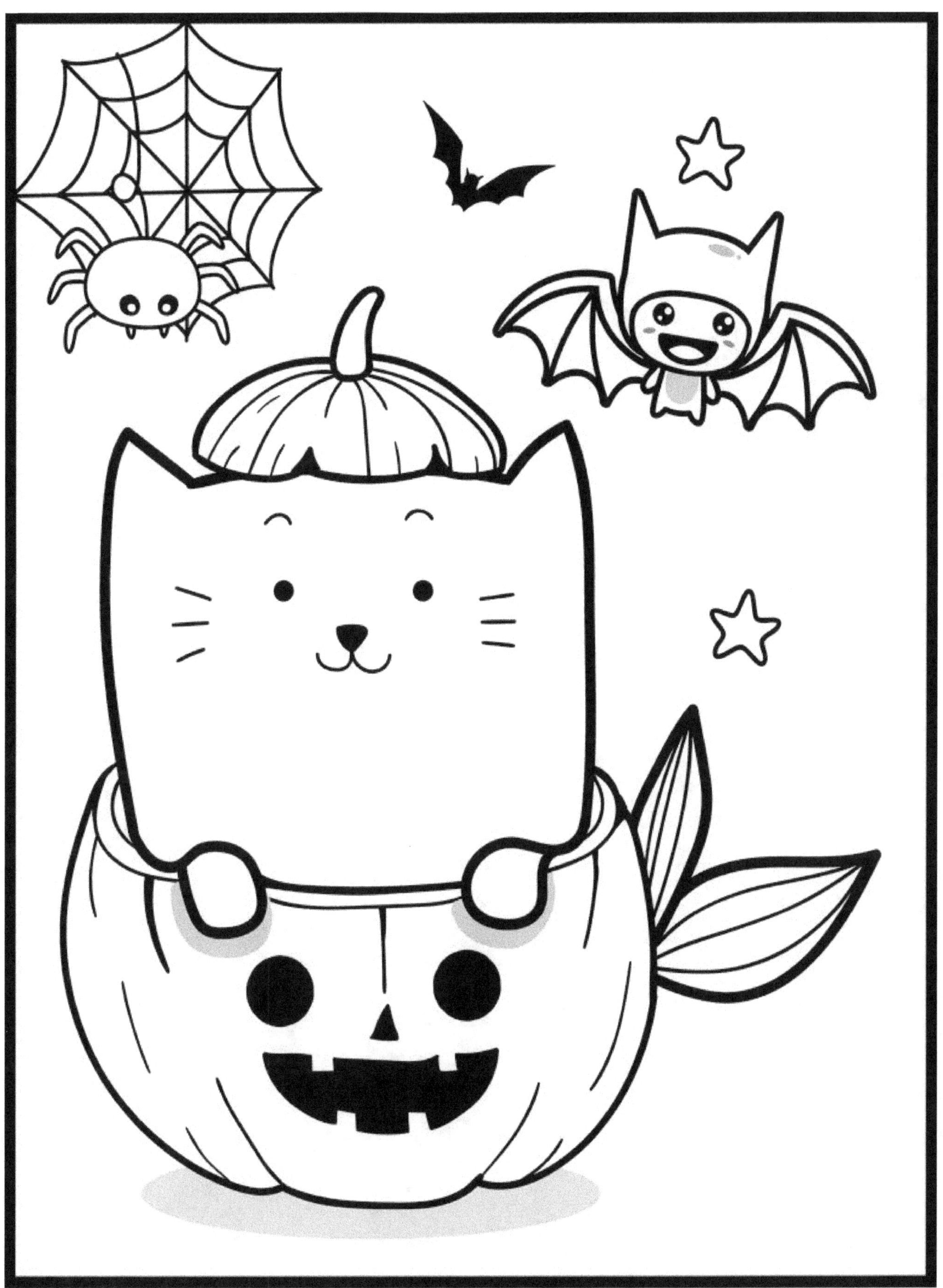

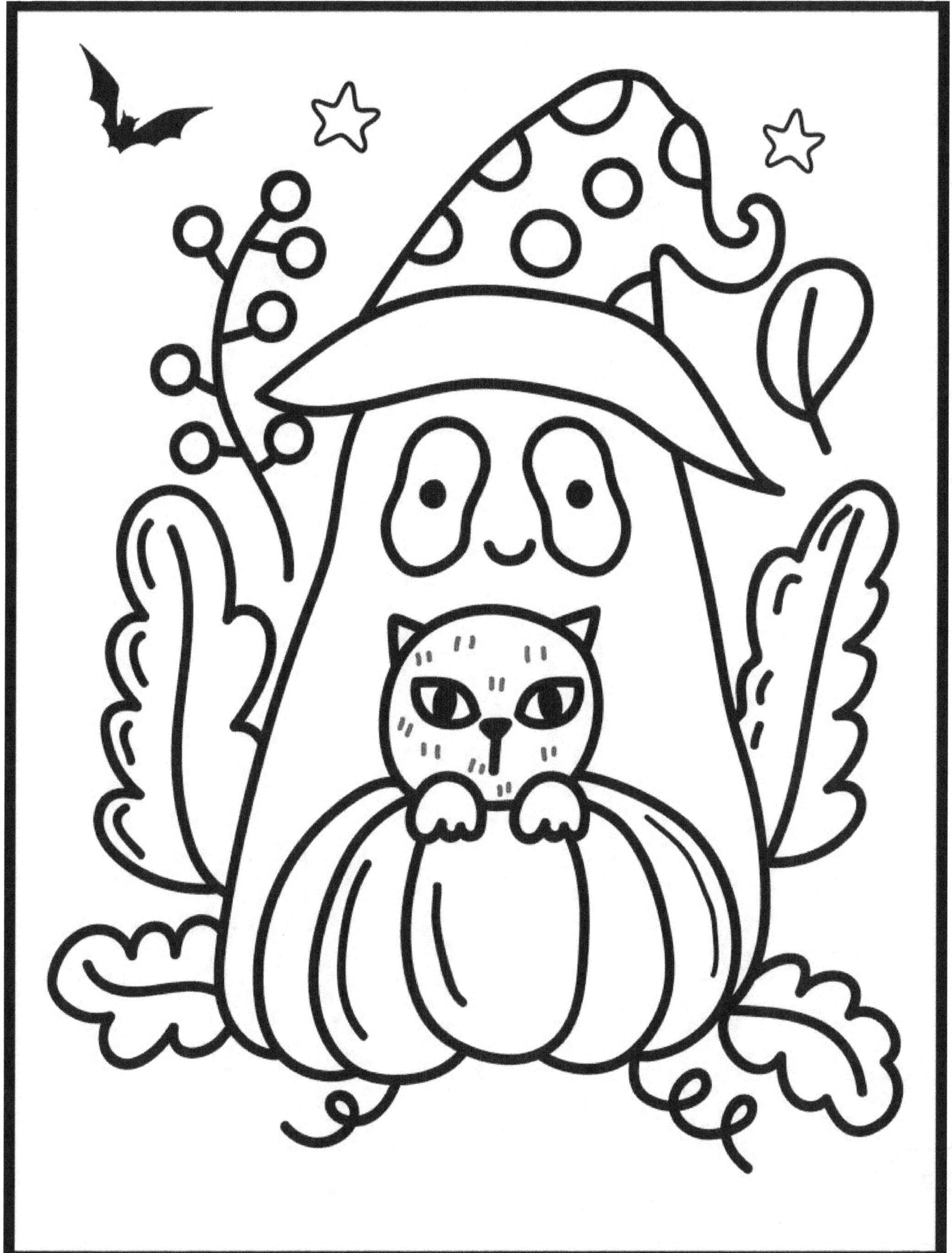

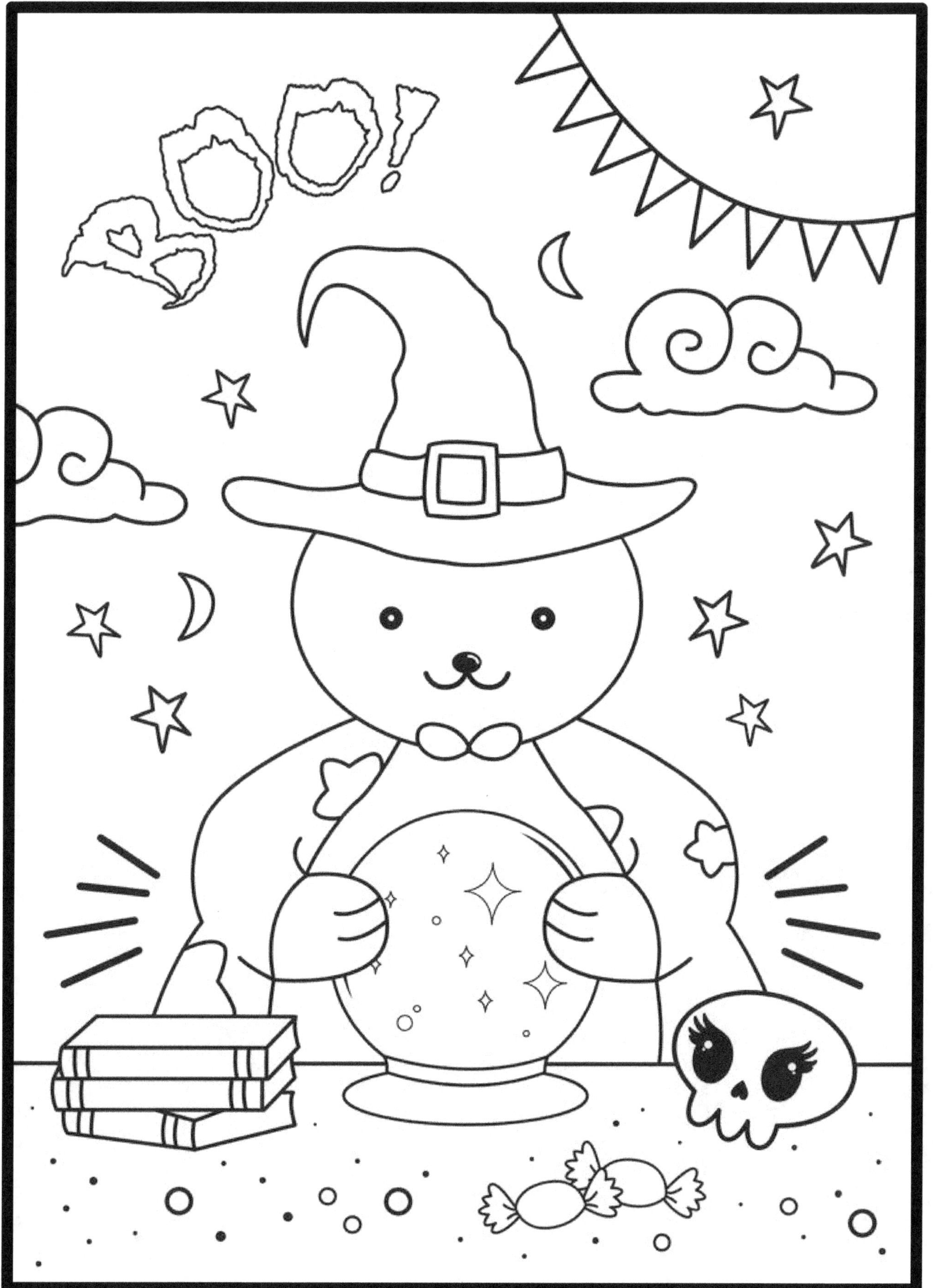
BOO!

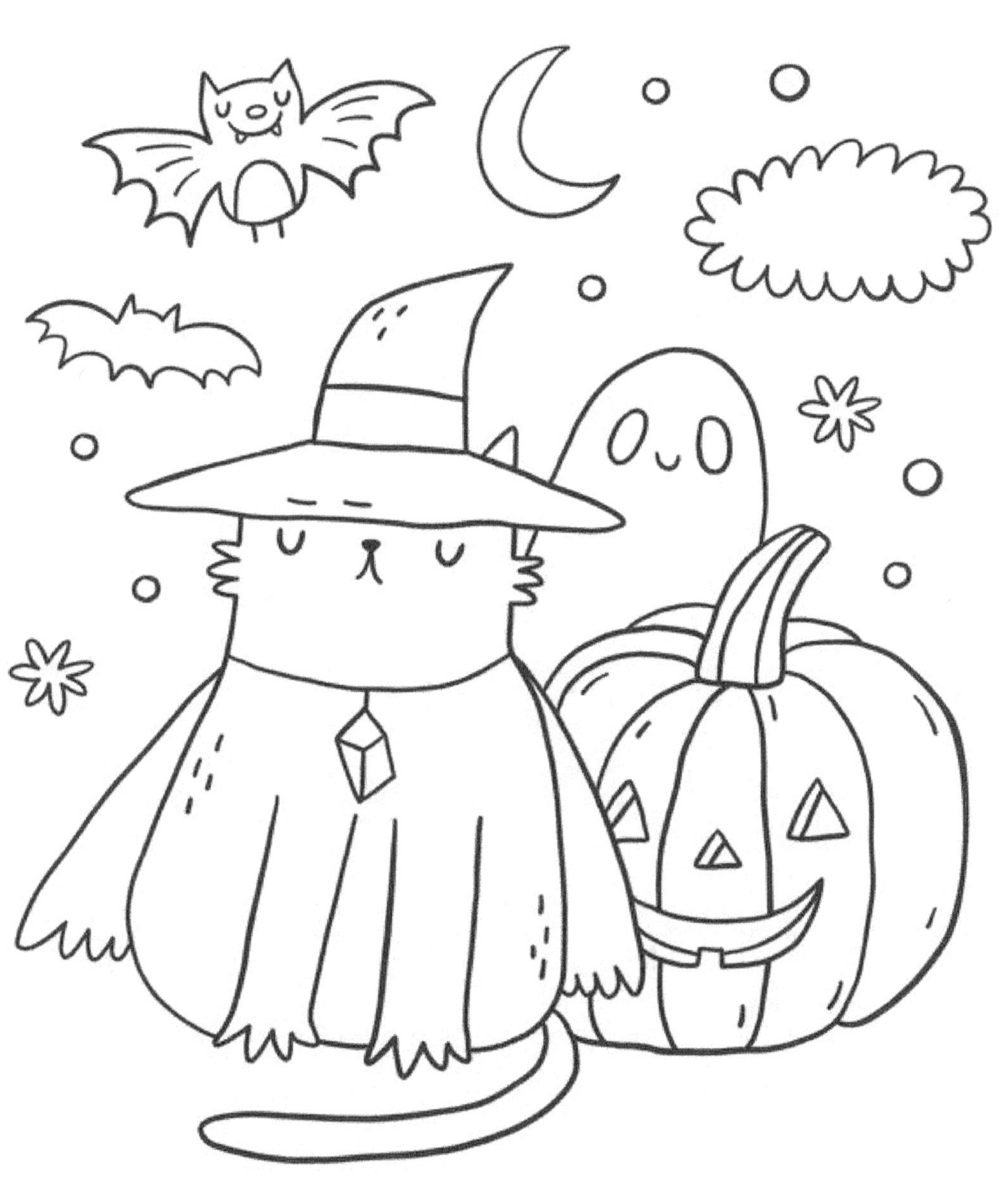

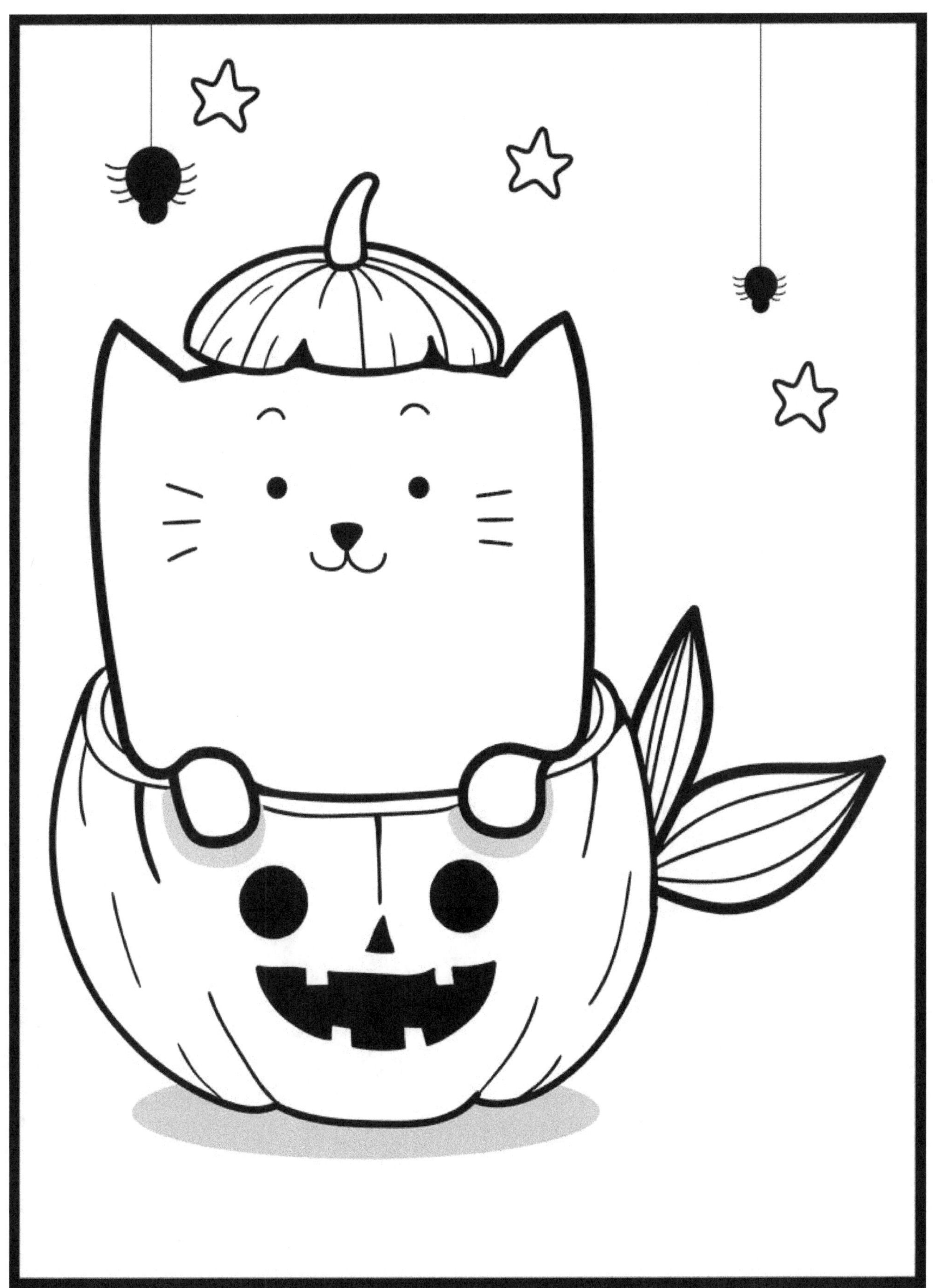

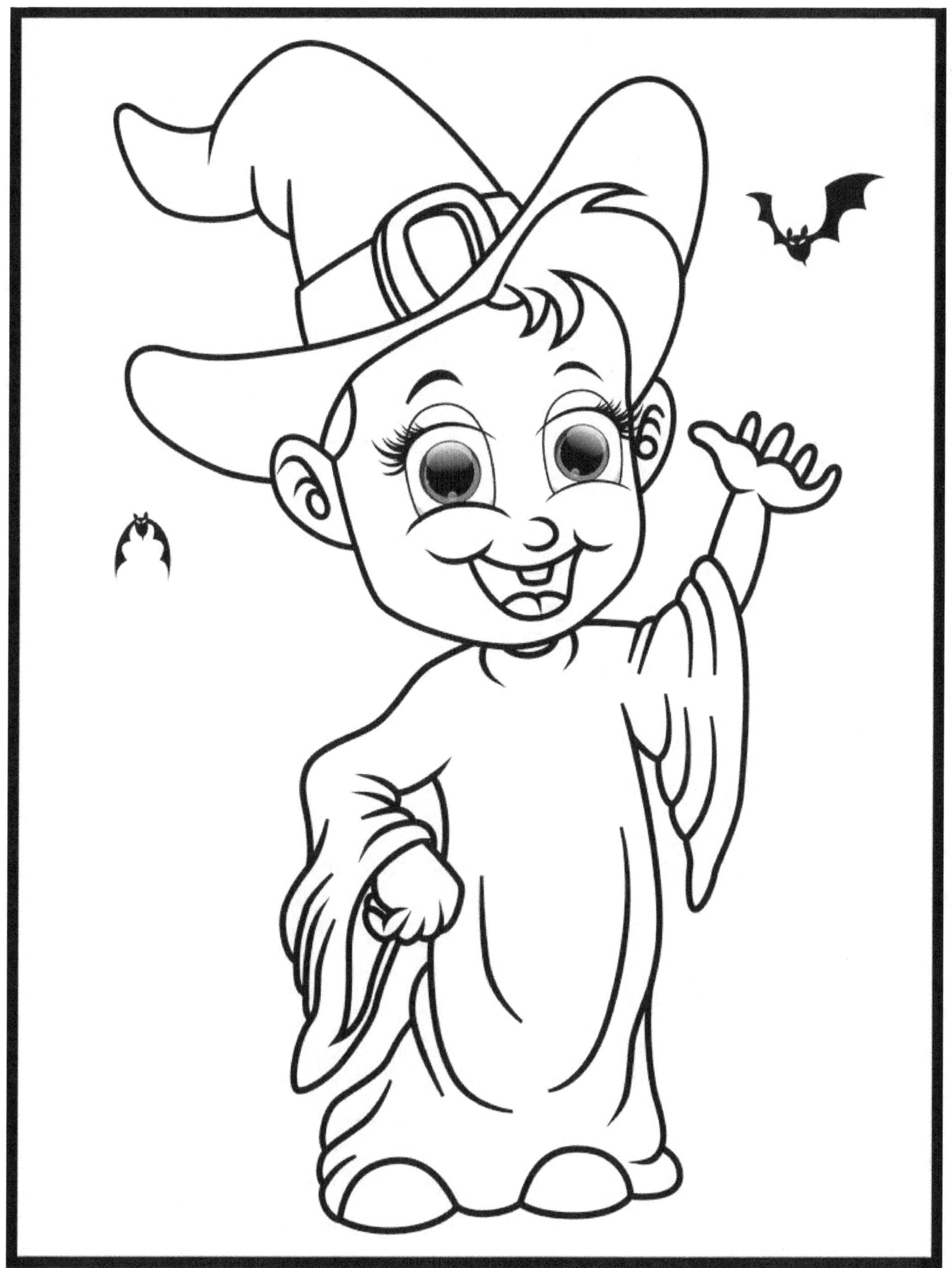

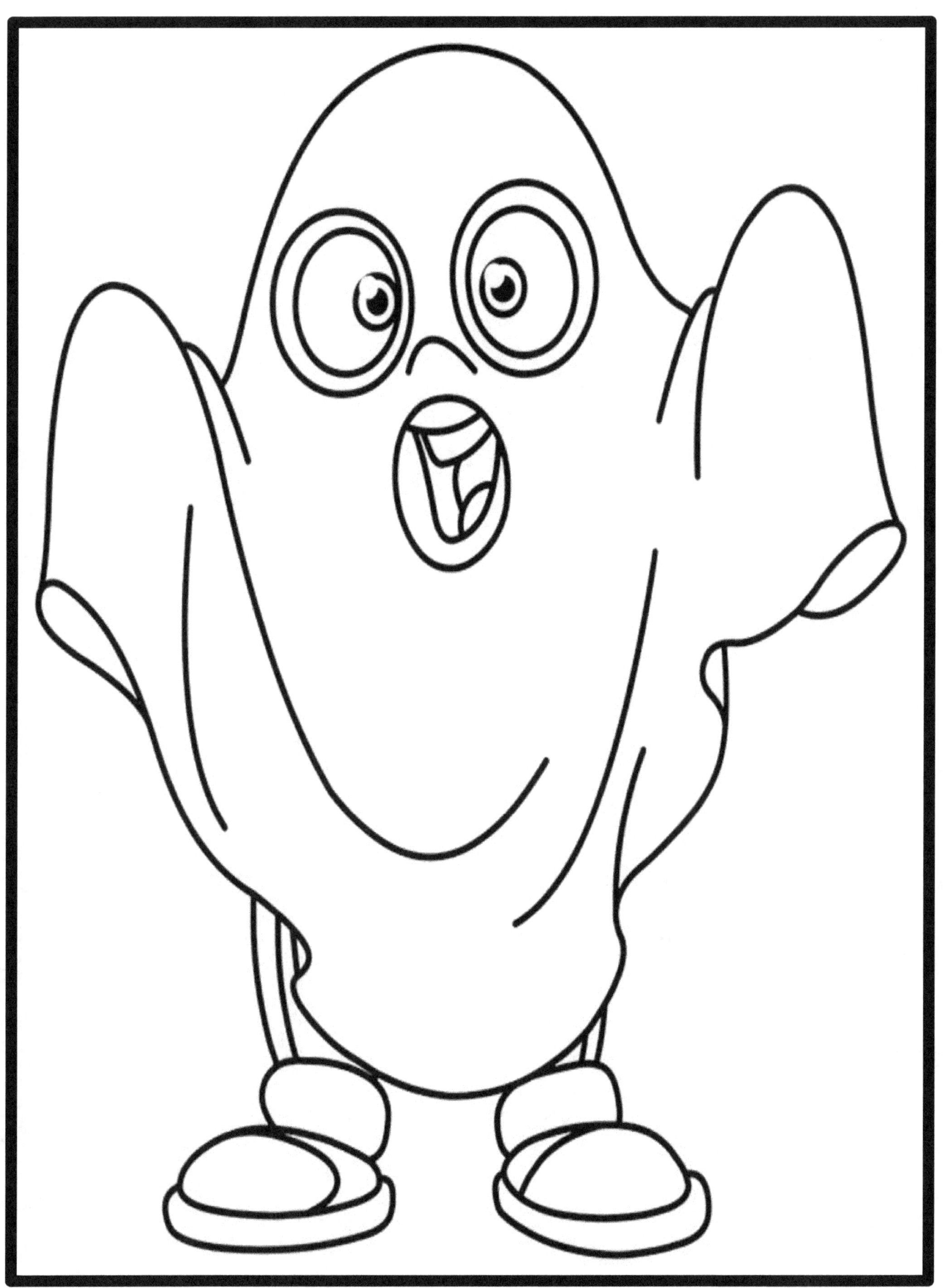

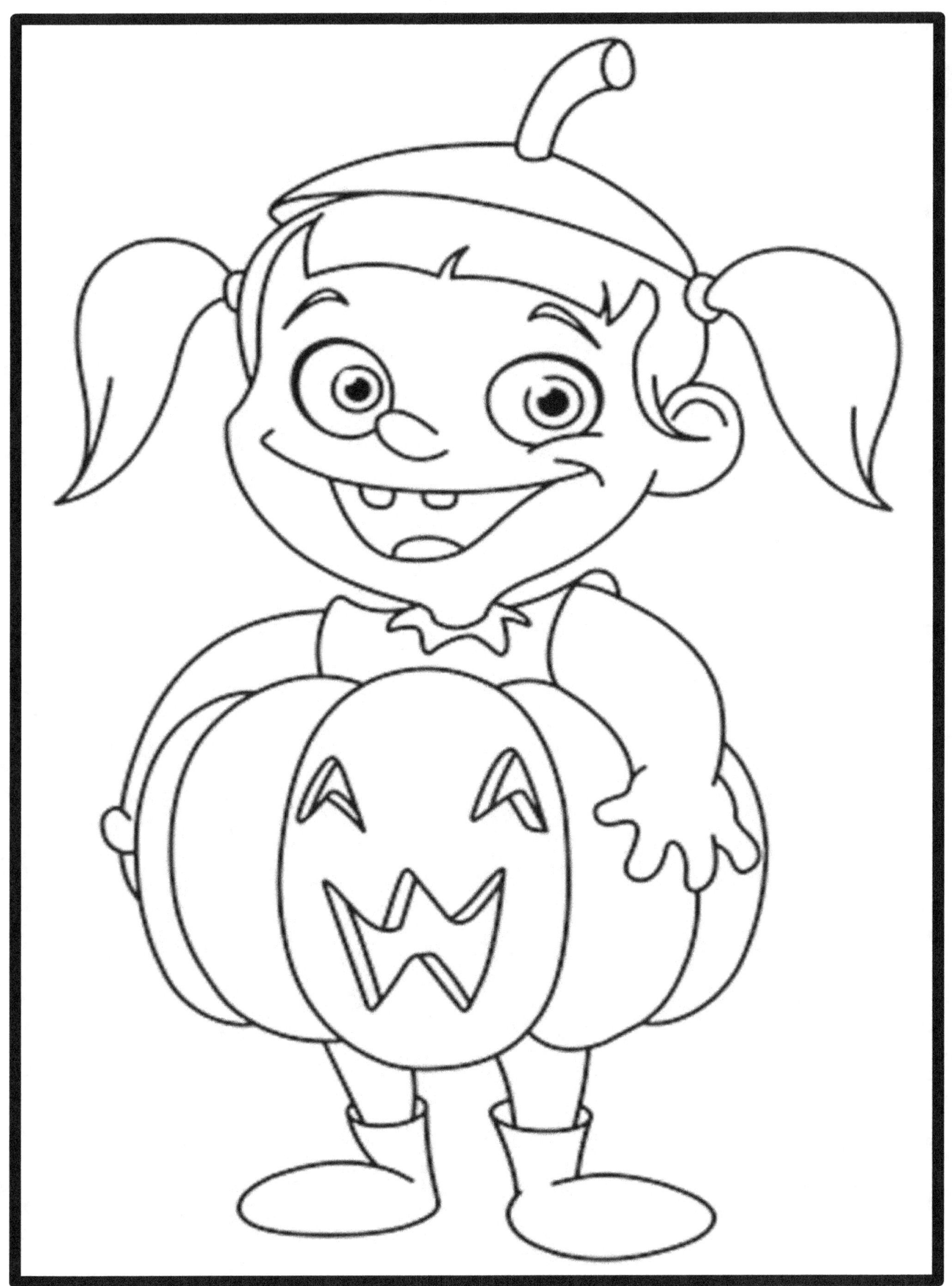

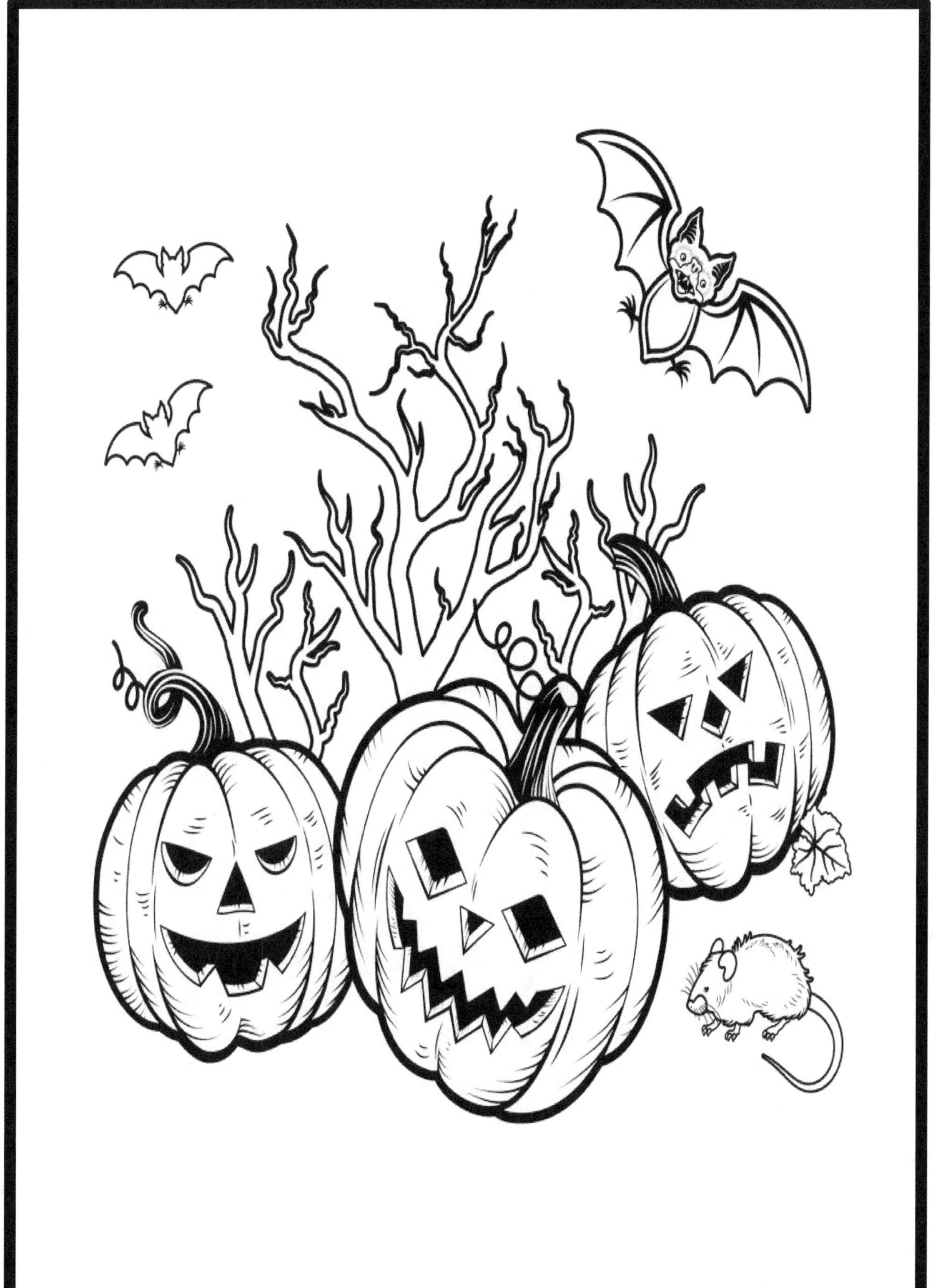

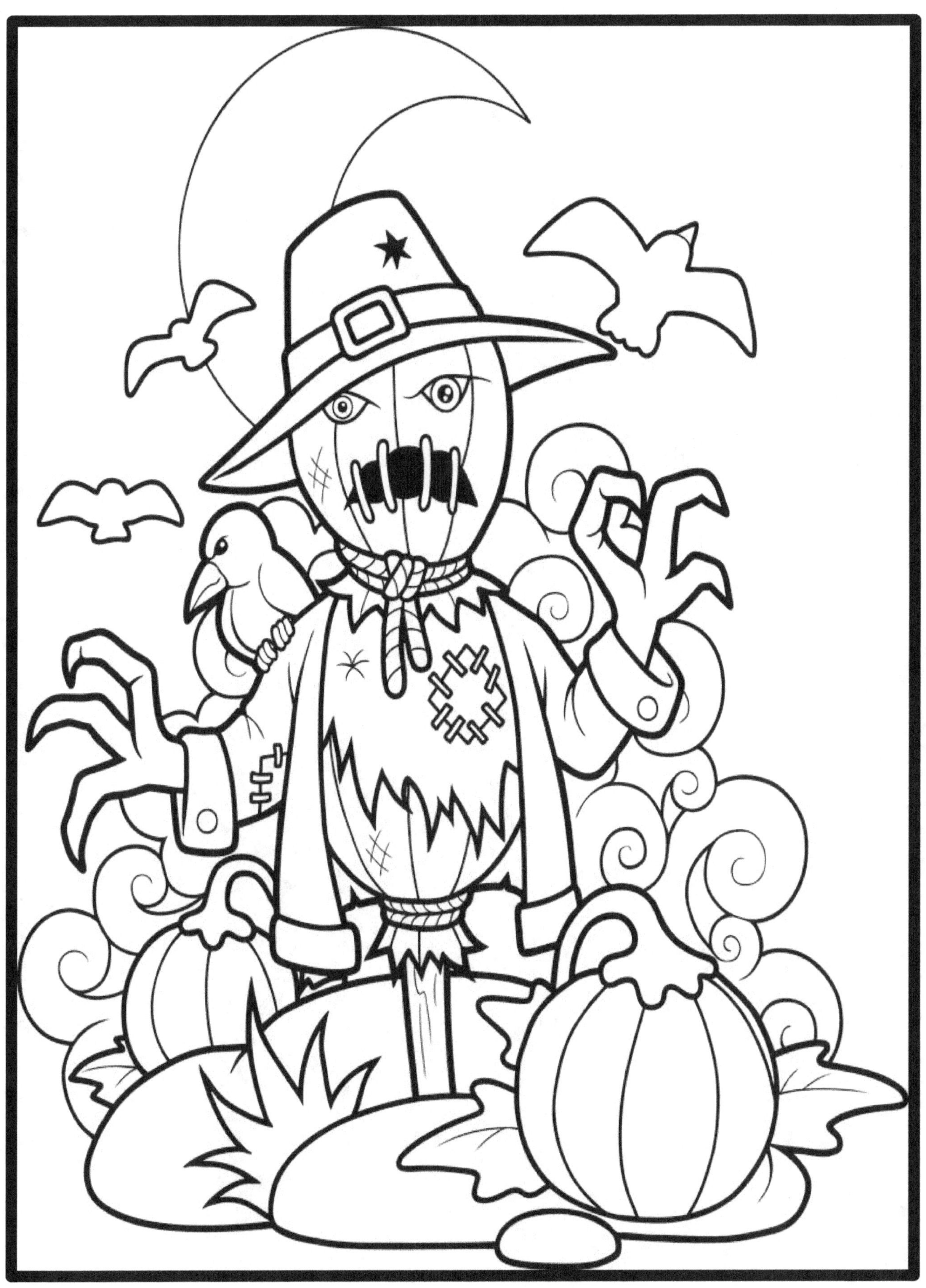

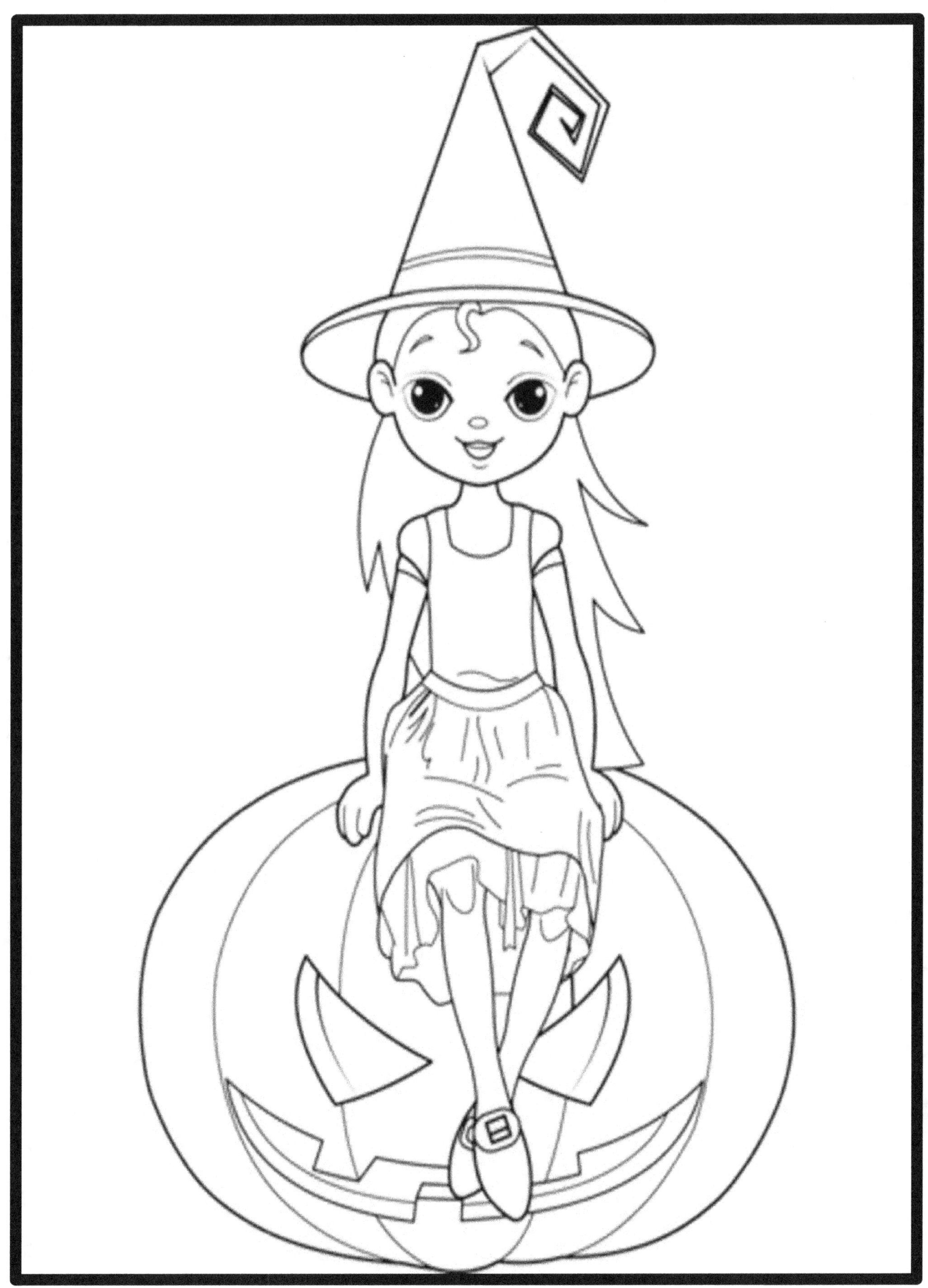

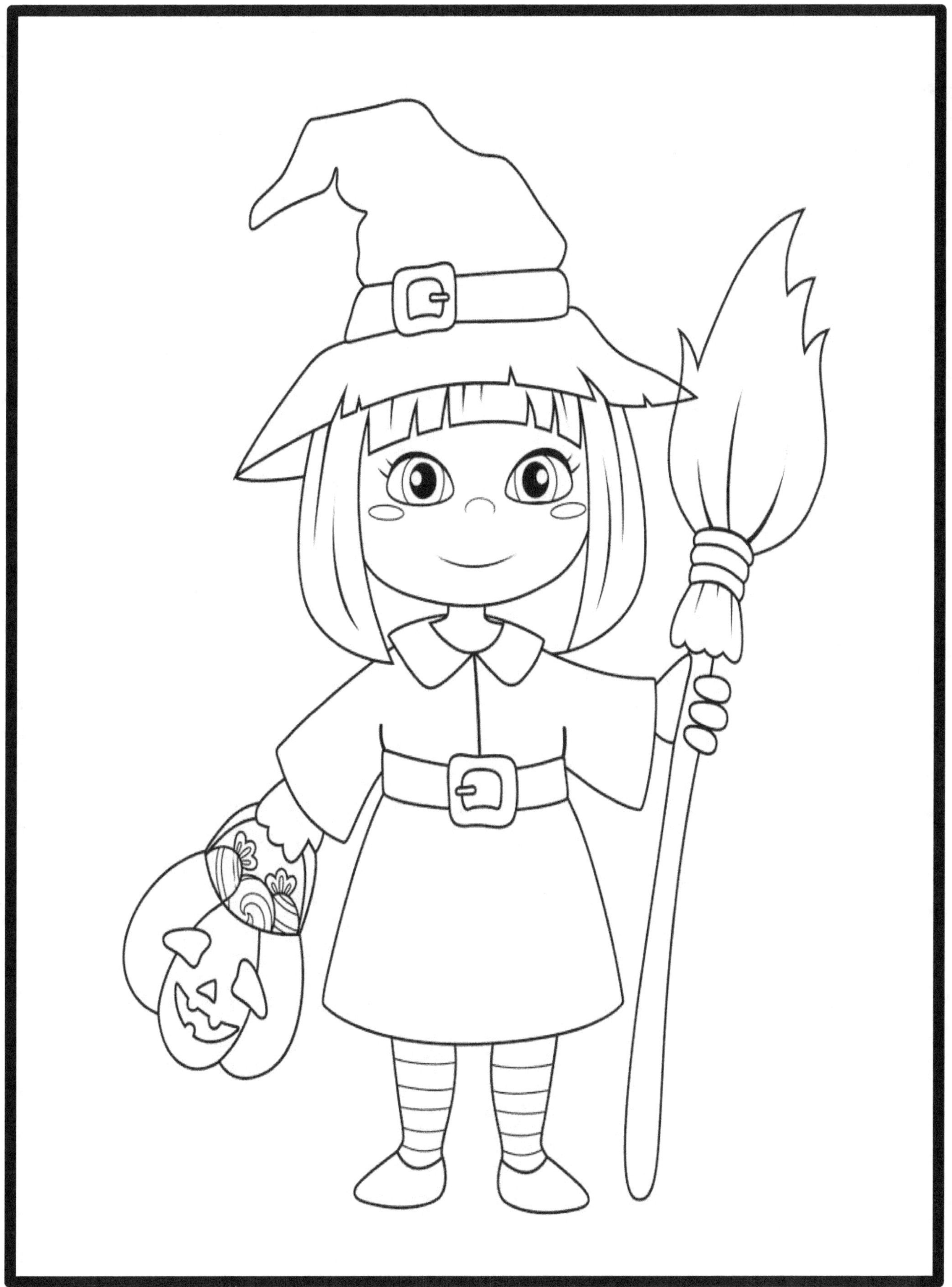

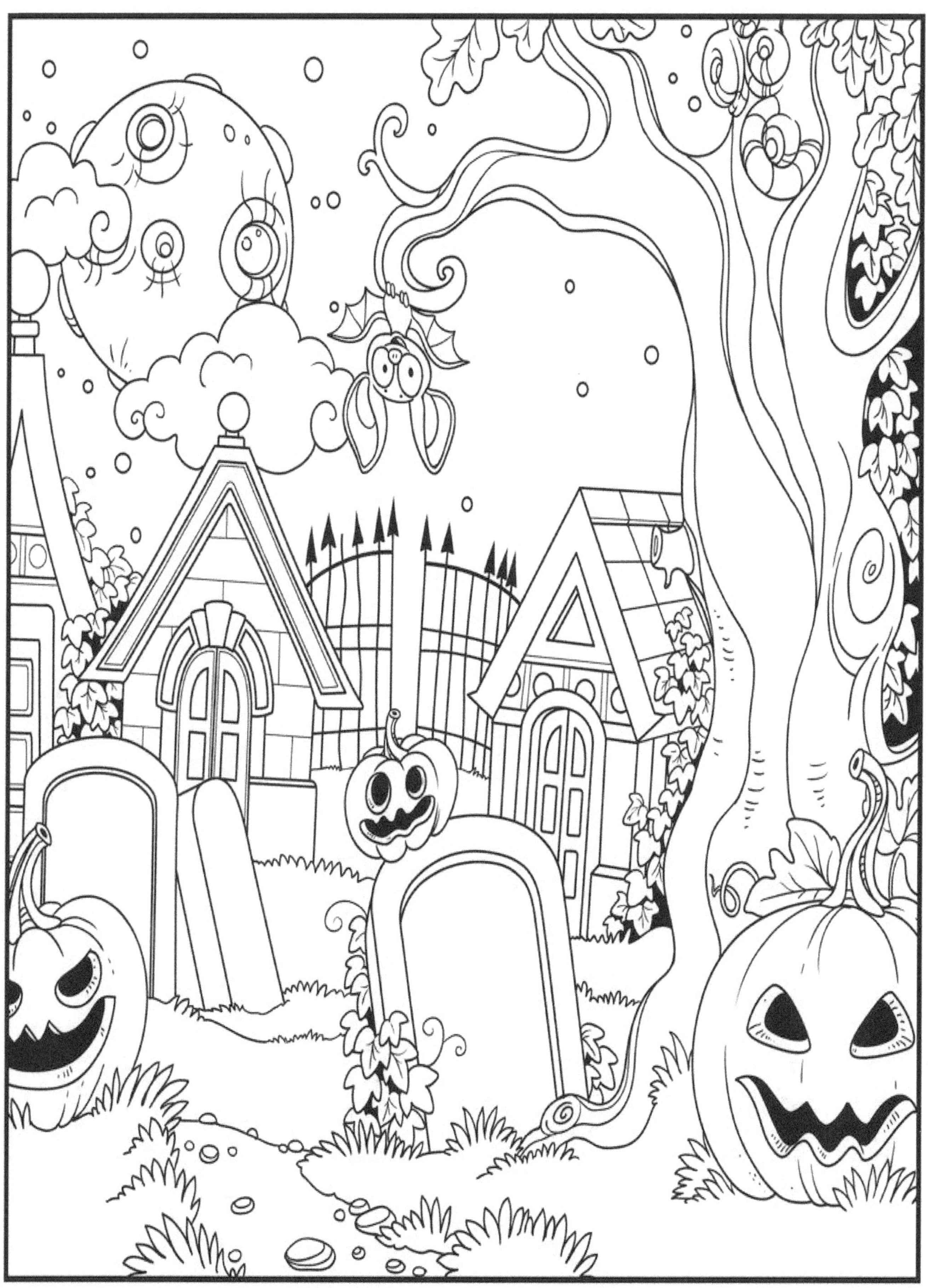

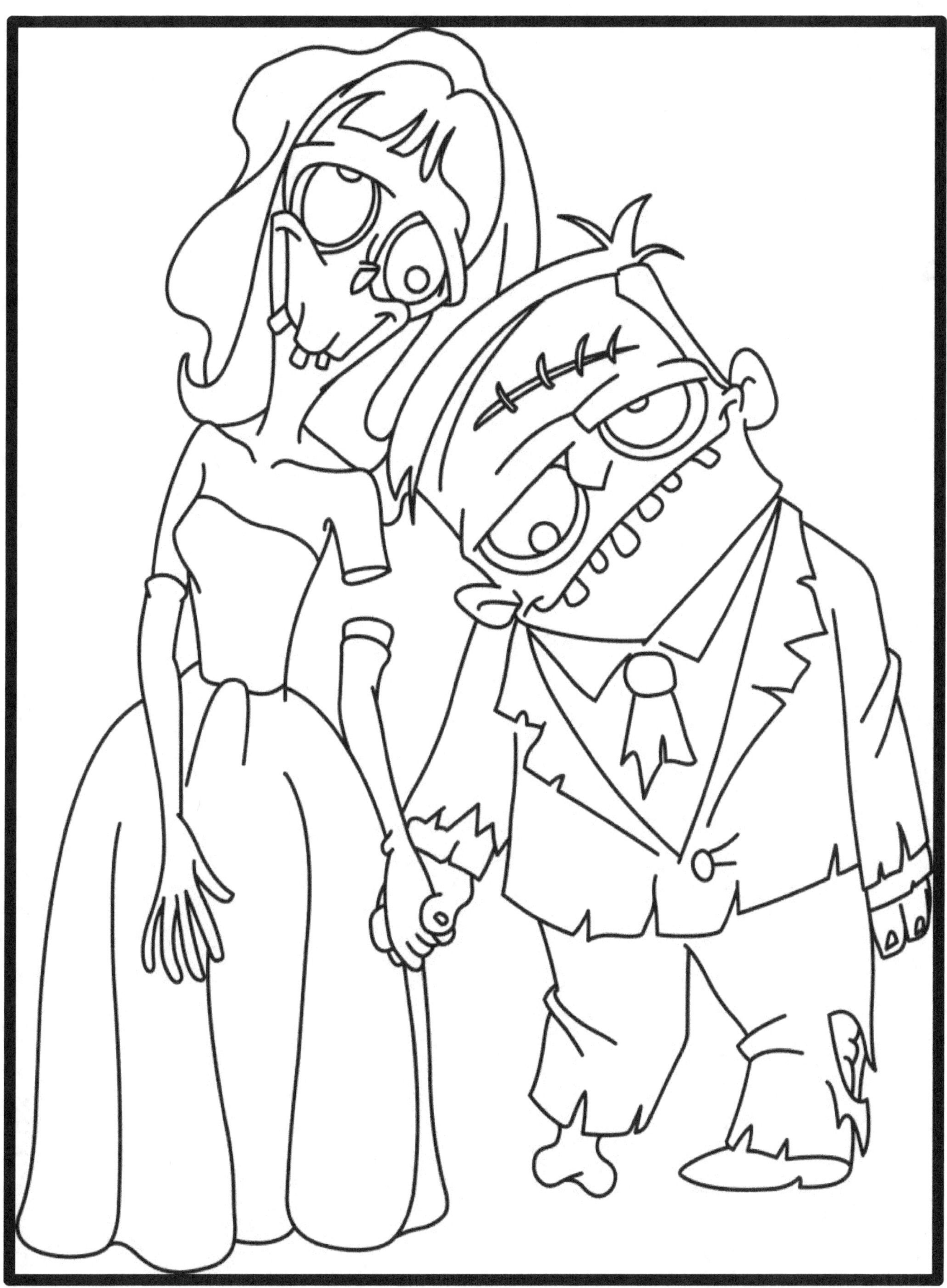

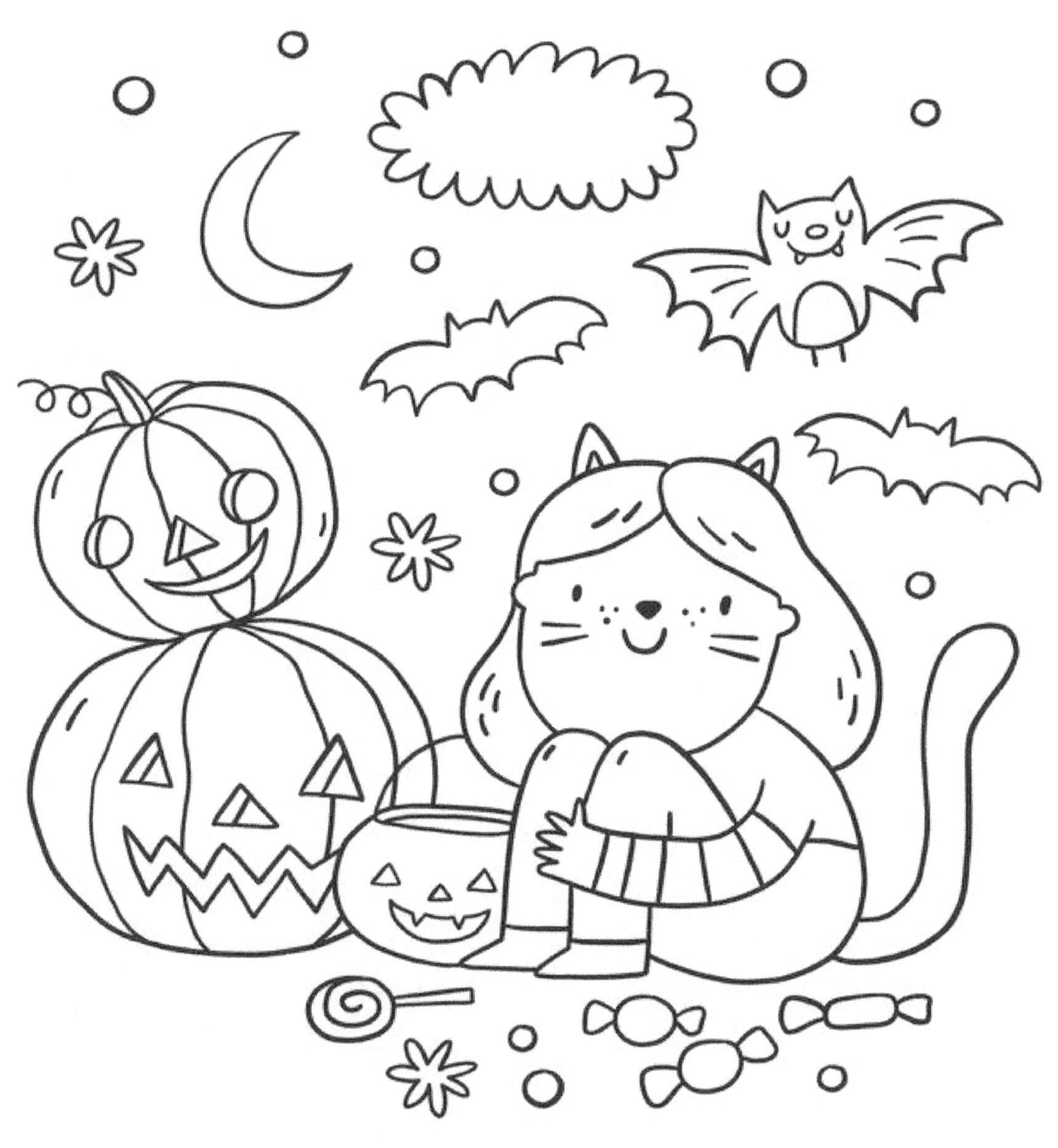

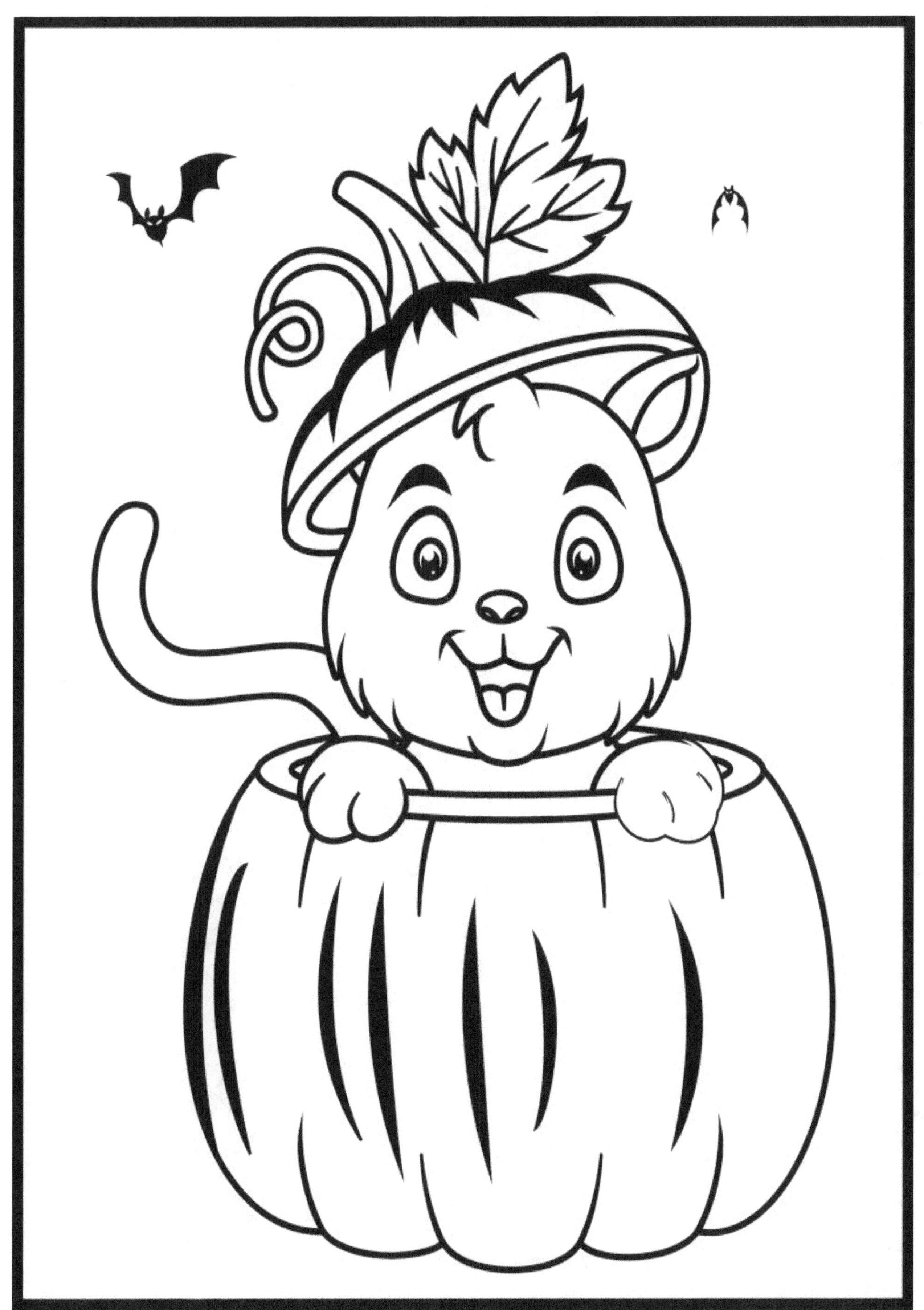

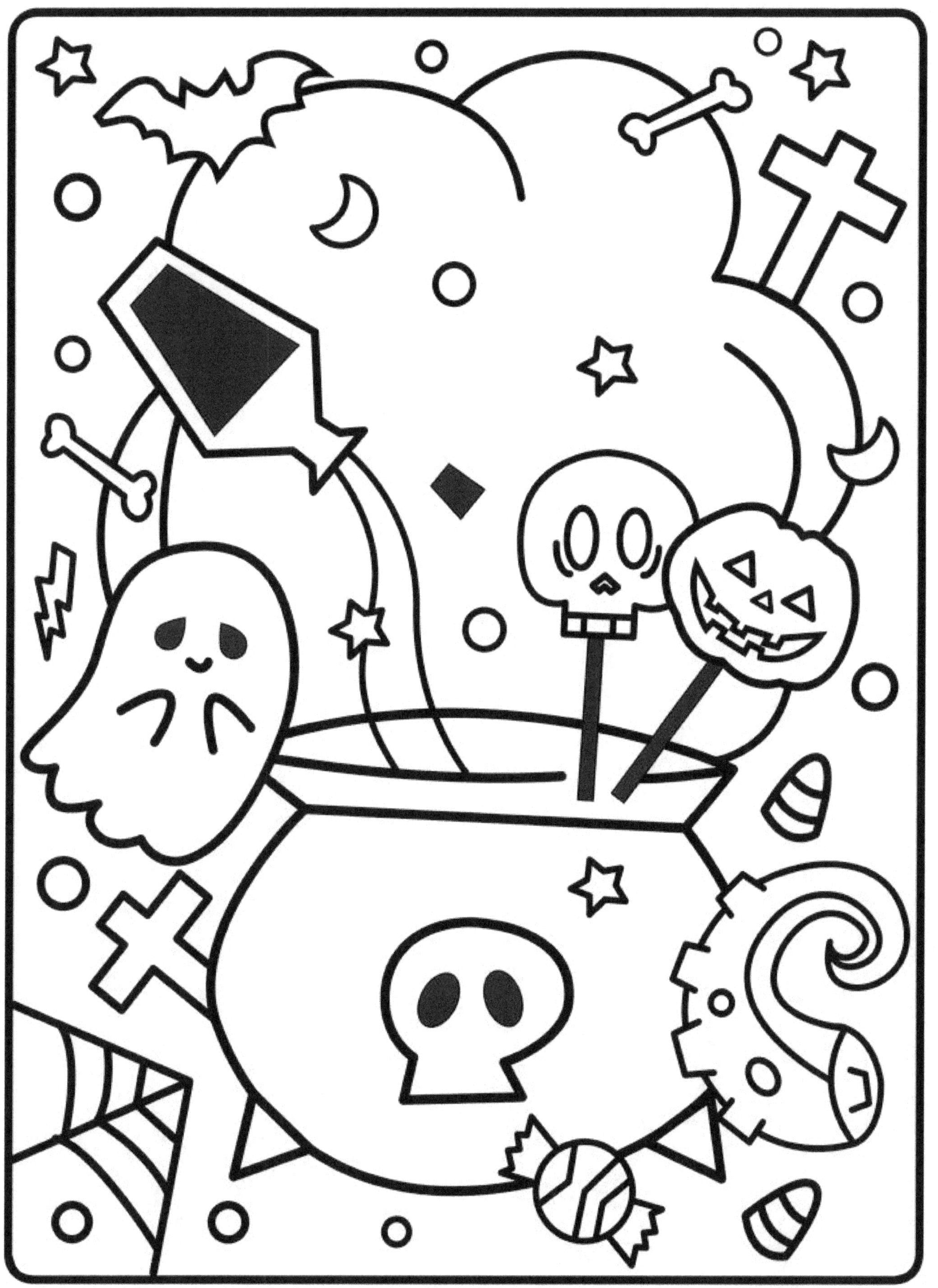

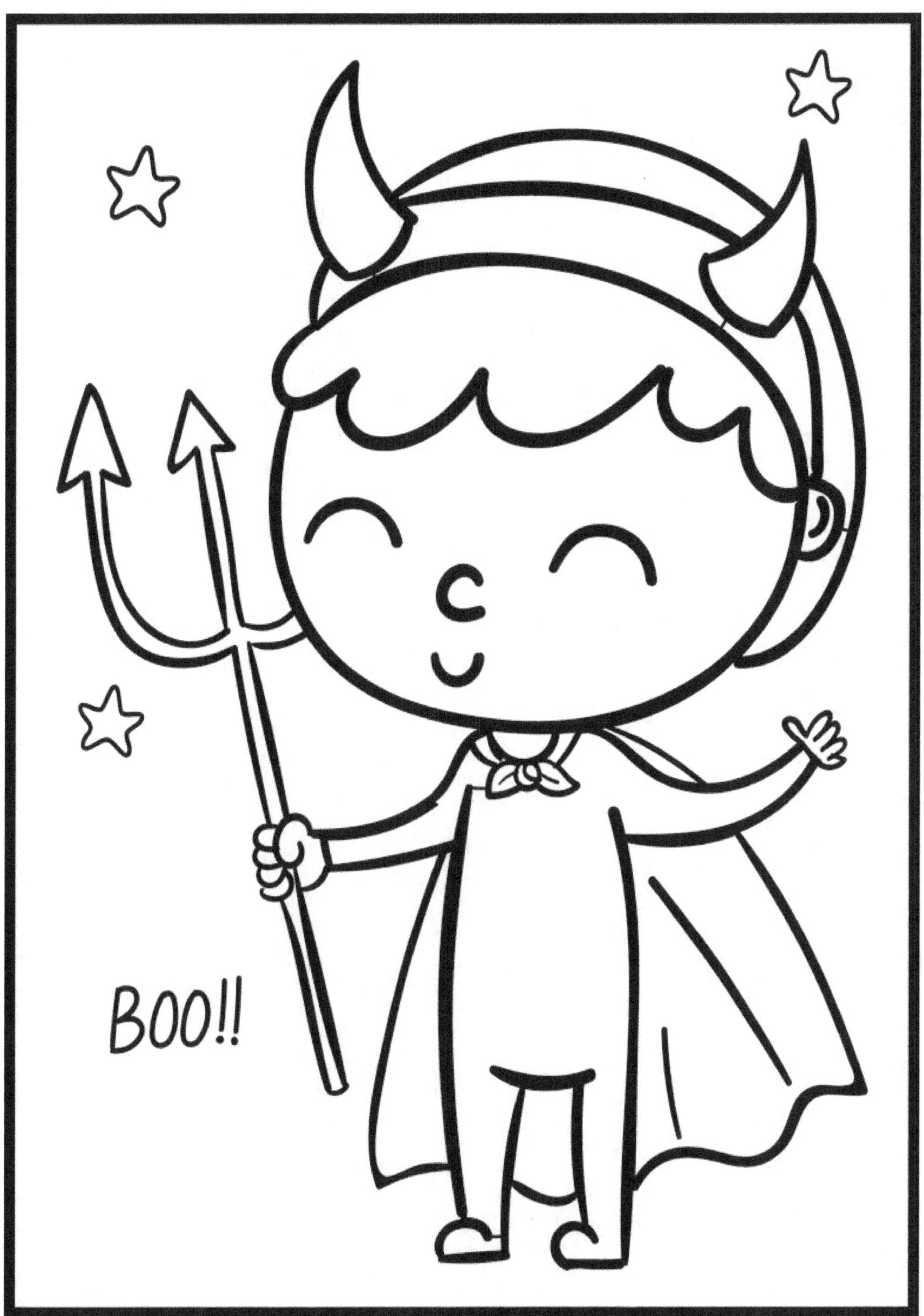
BOO!!

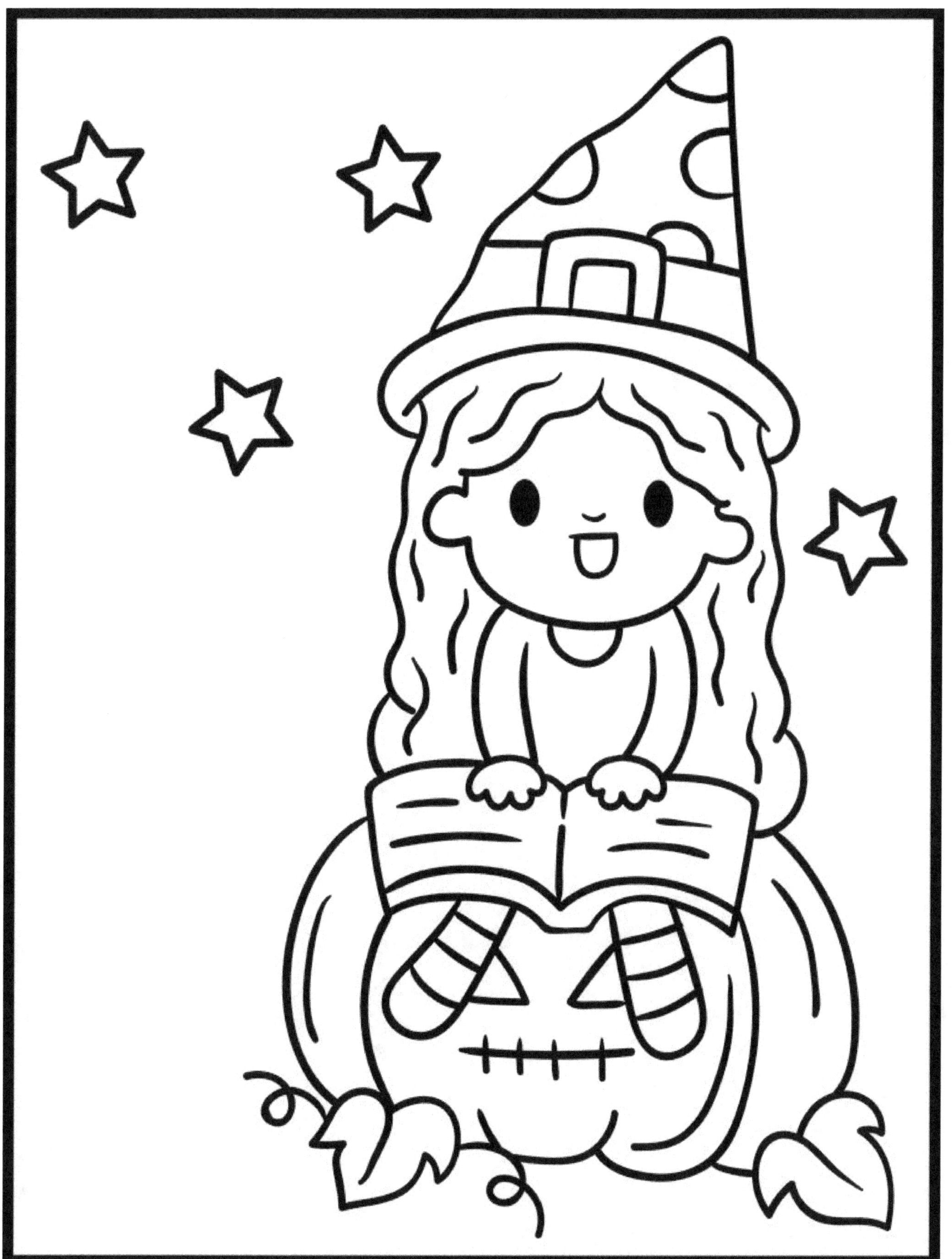

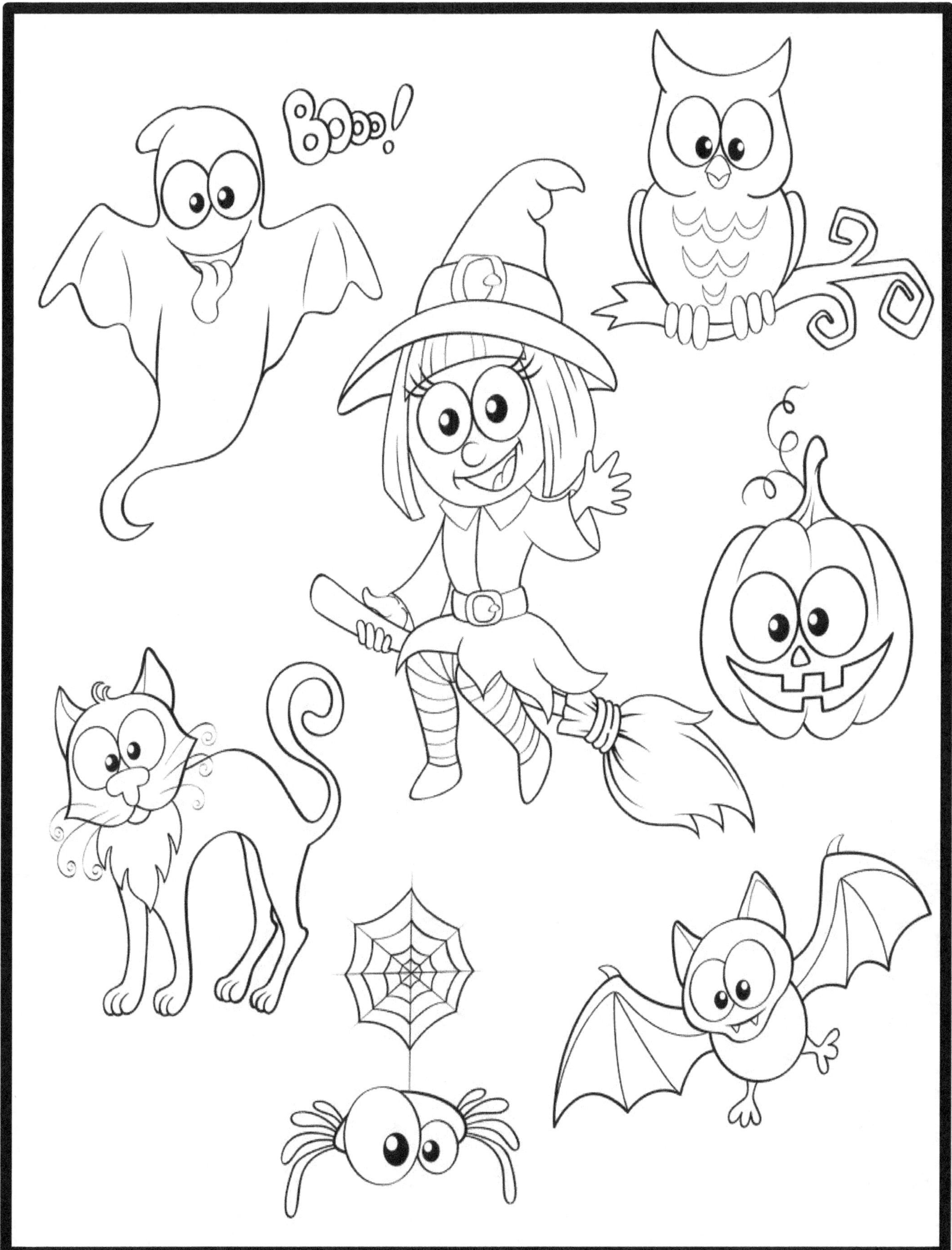
Booo!

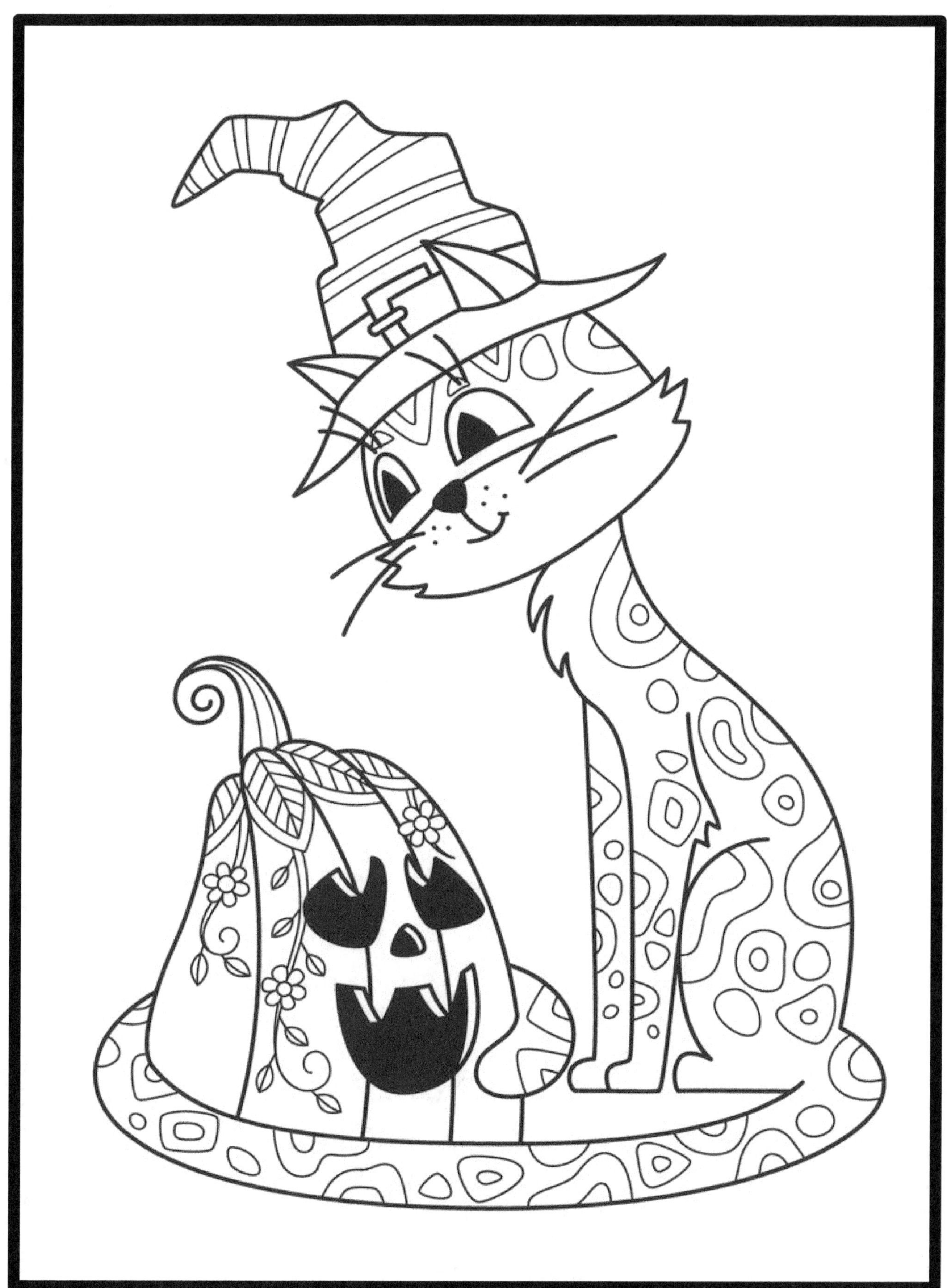

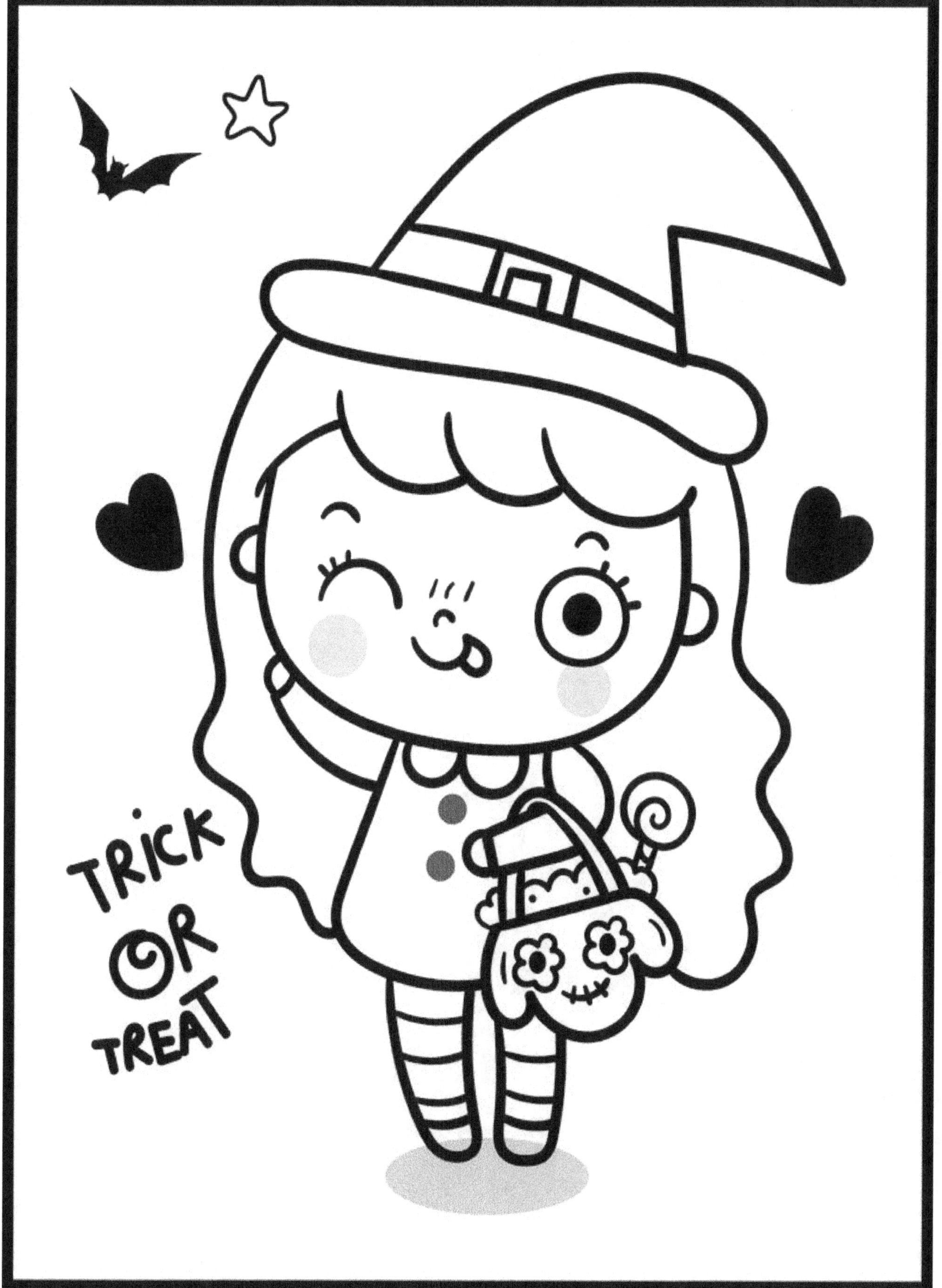
TRICK
OR
TREAT

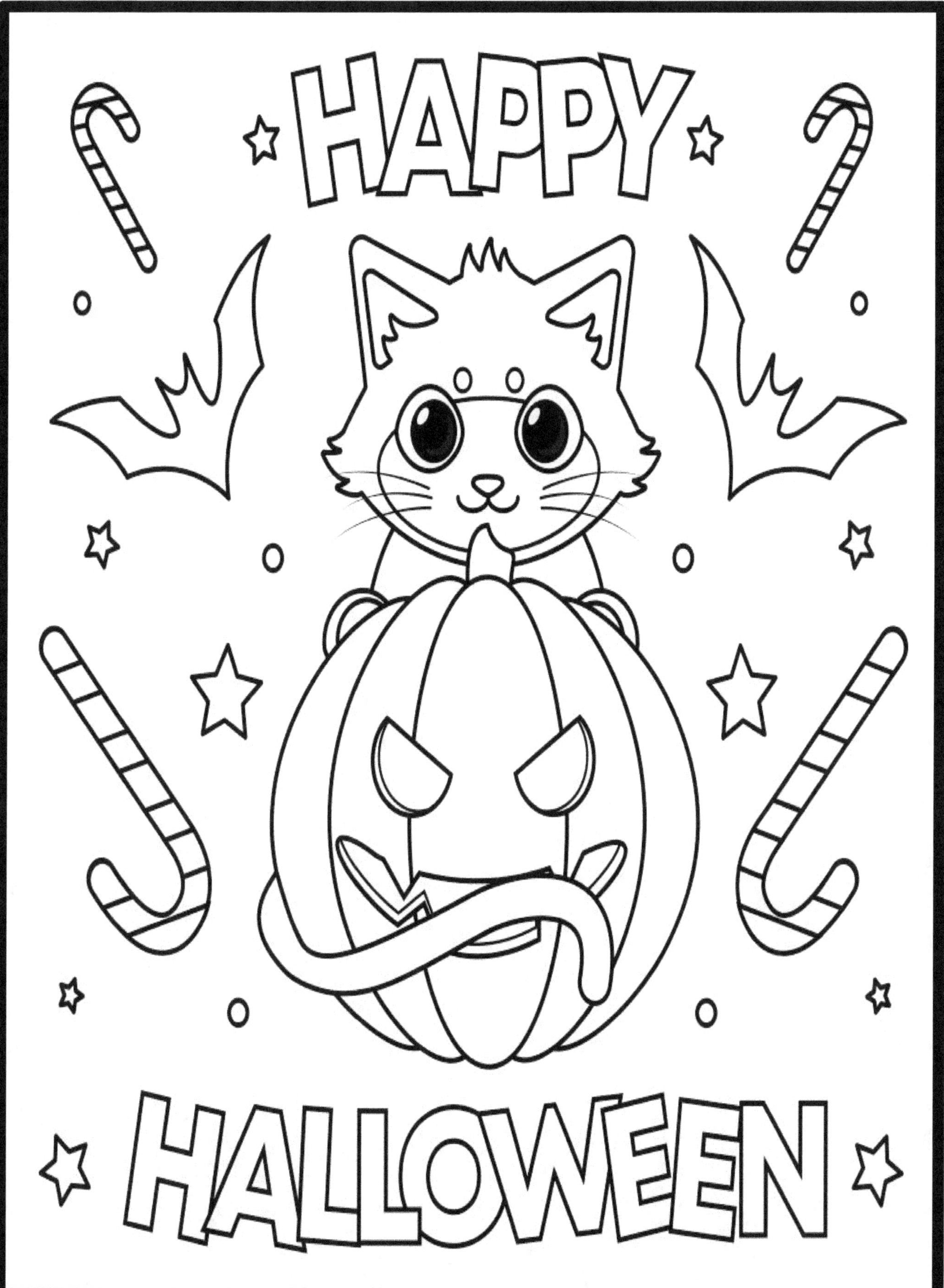

HAPPY
HALLOWEEN

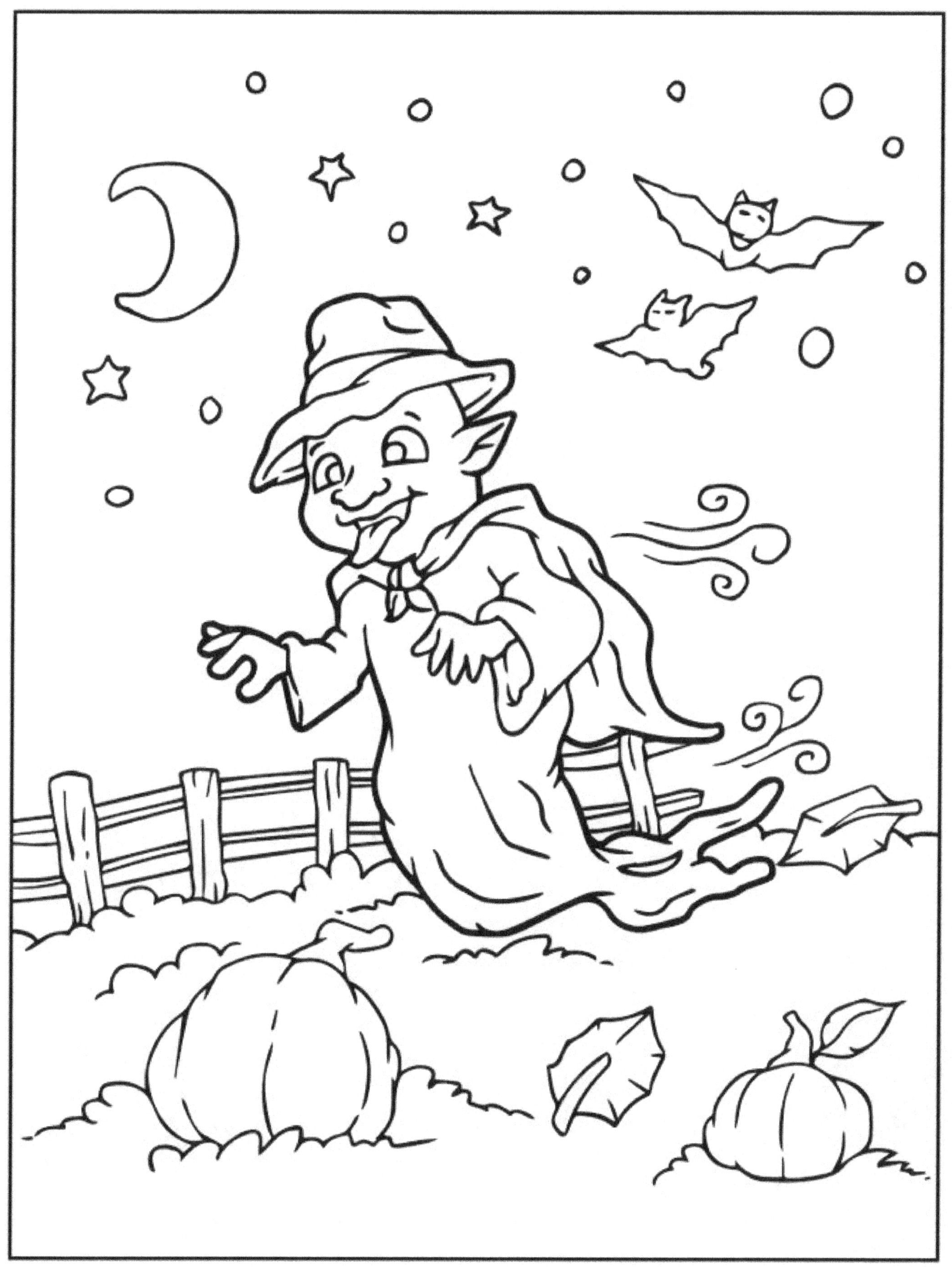

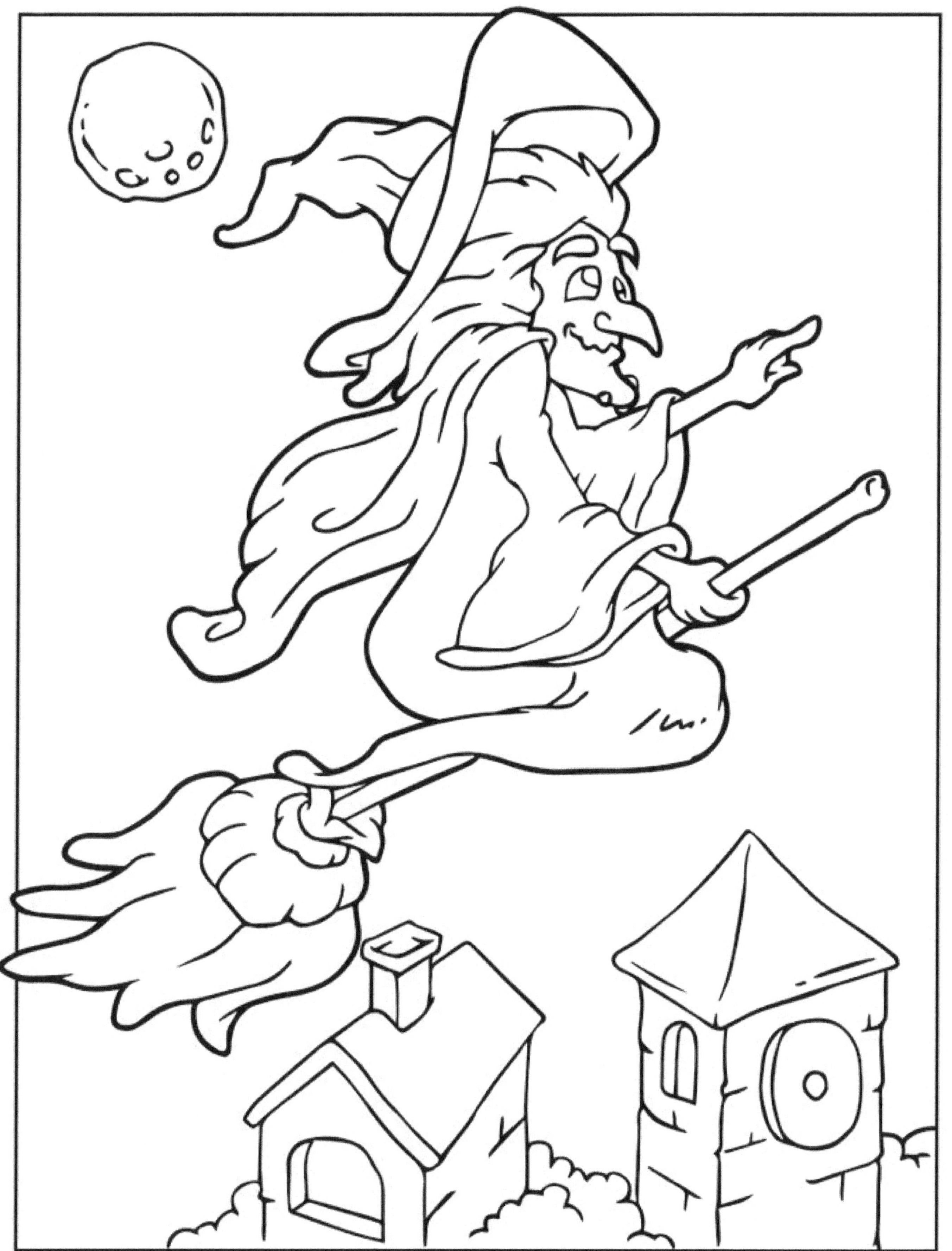

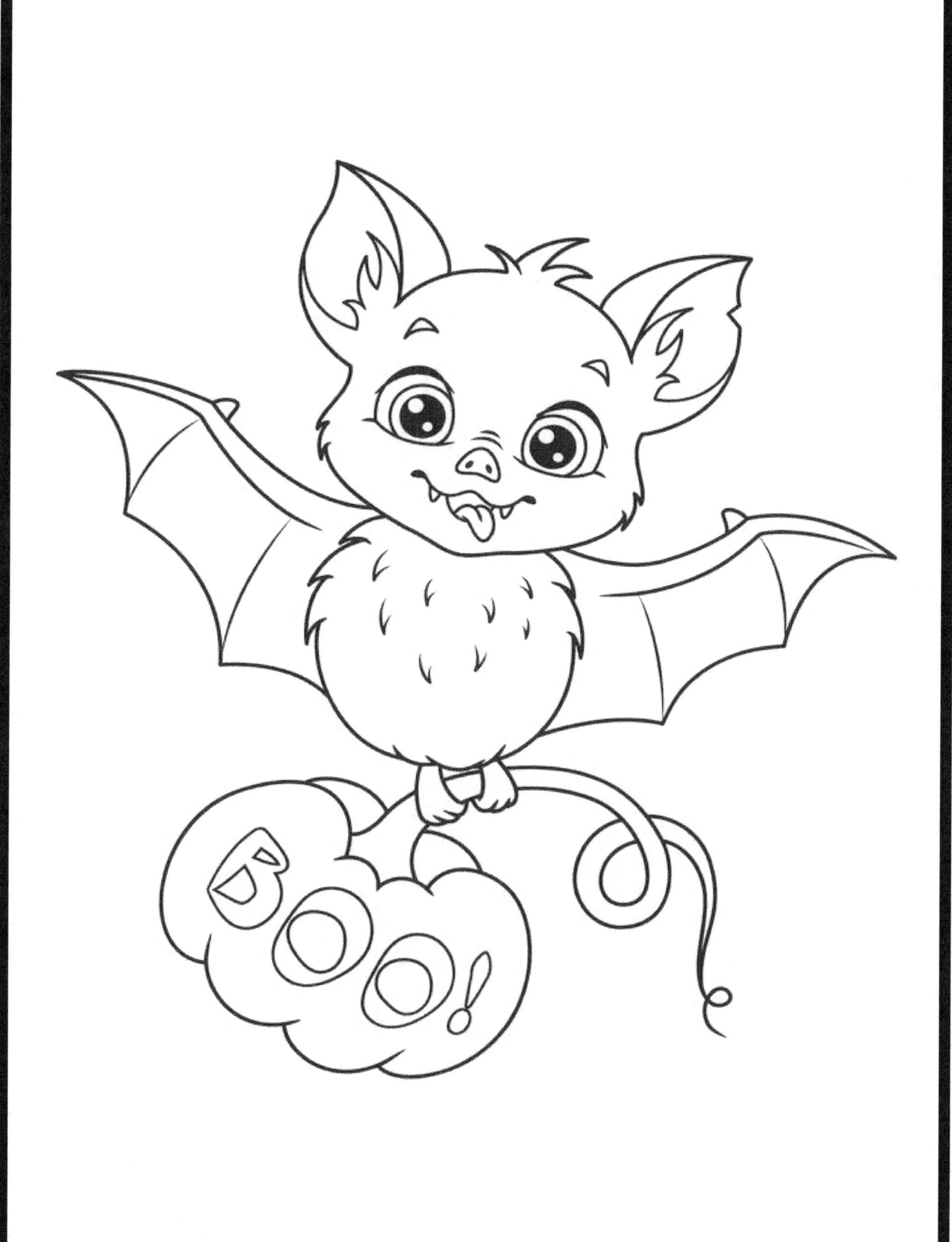

BOO!

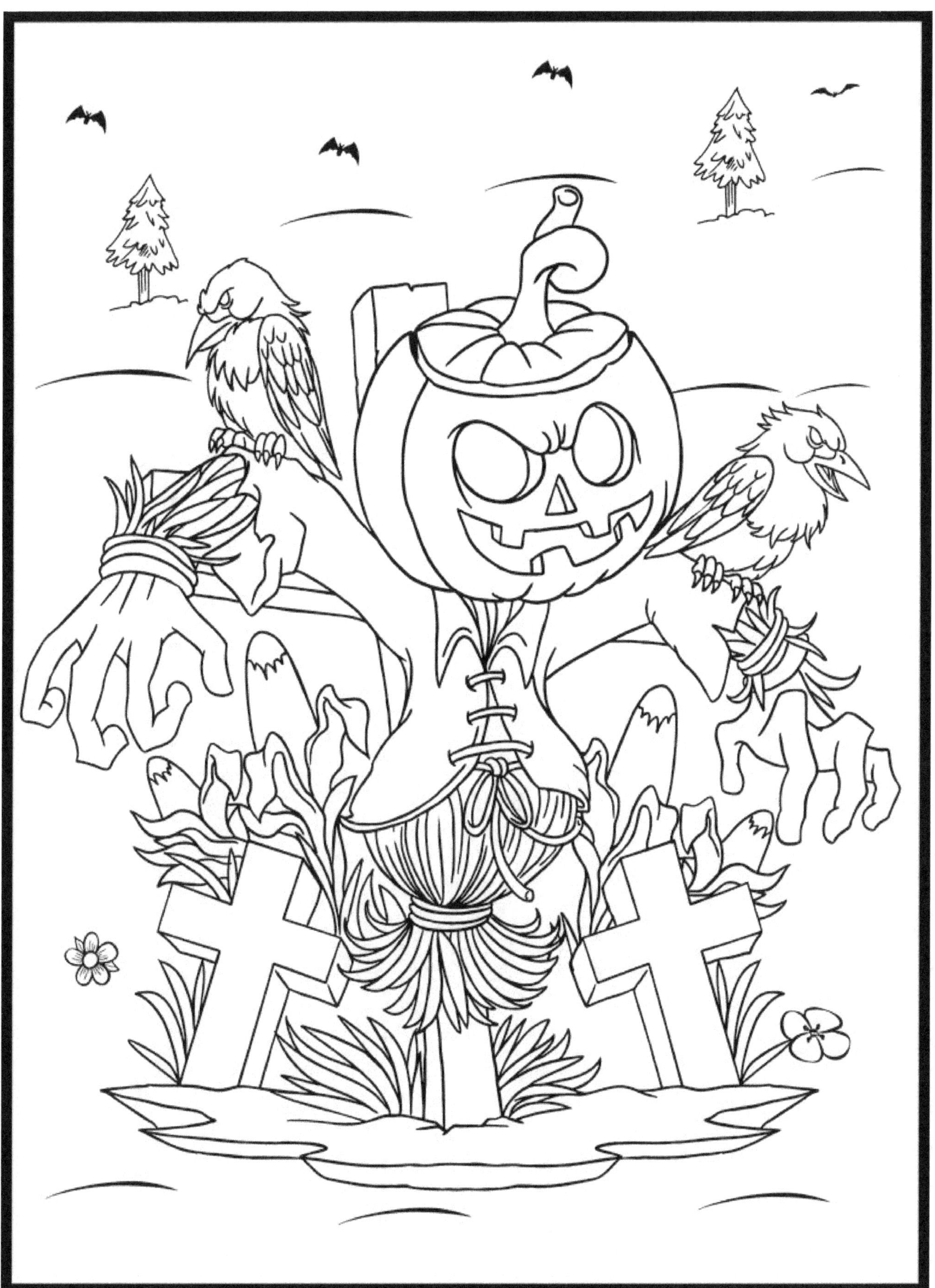

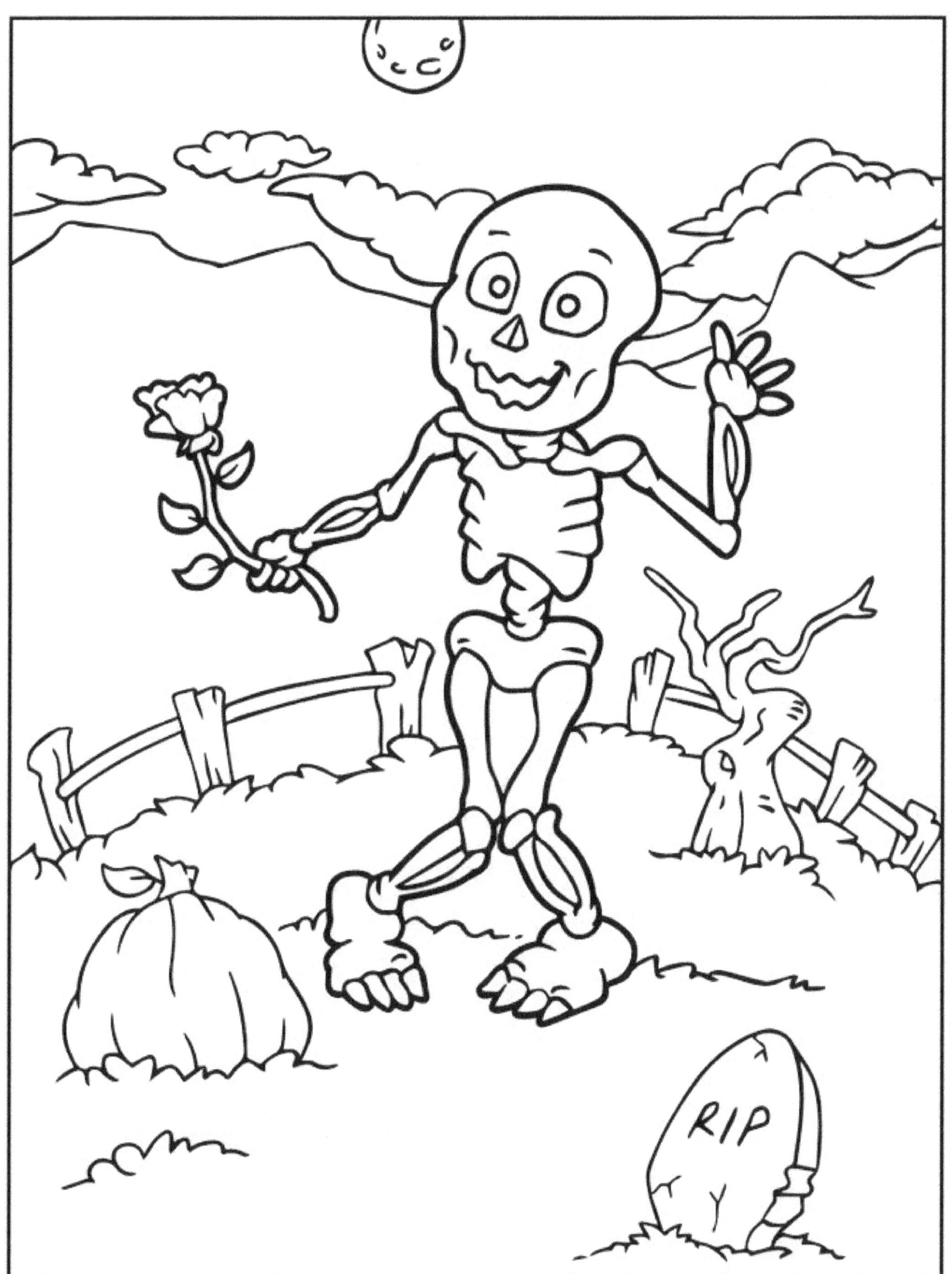
RIP

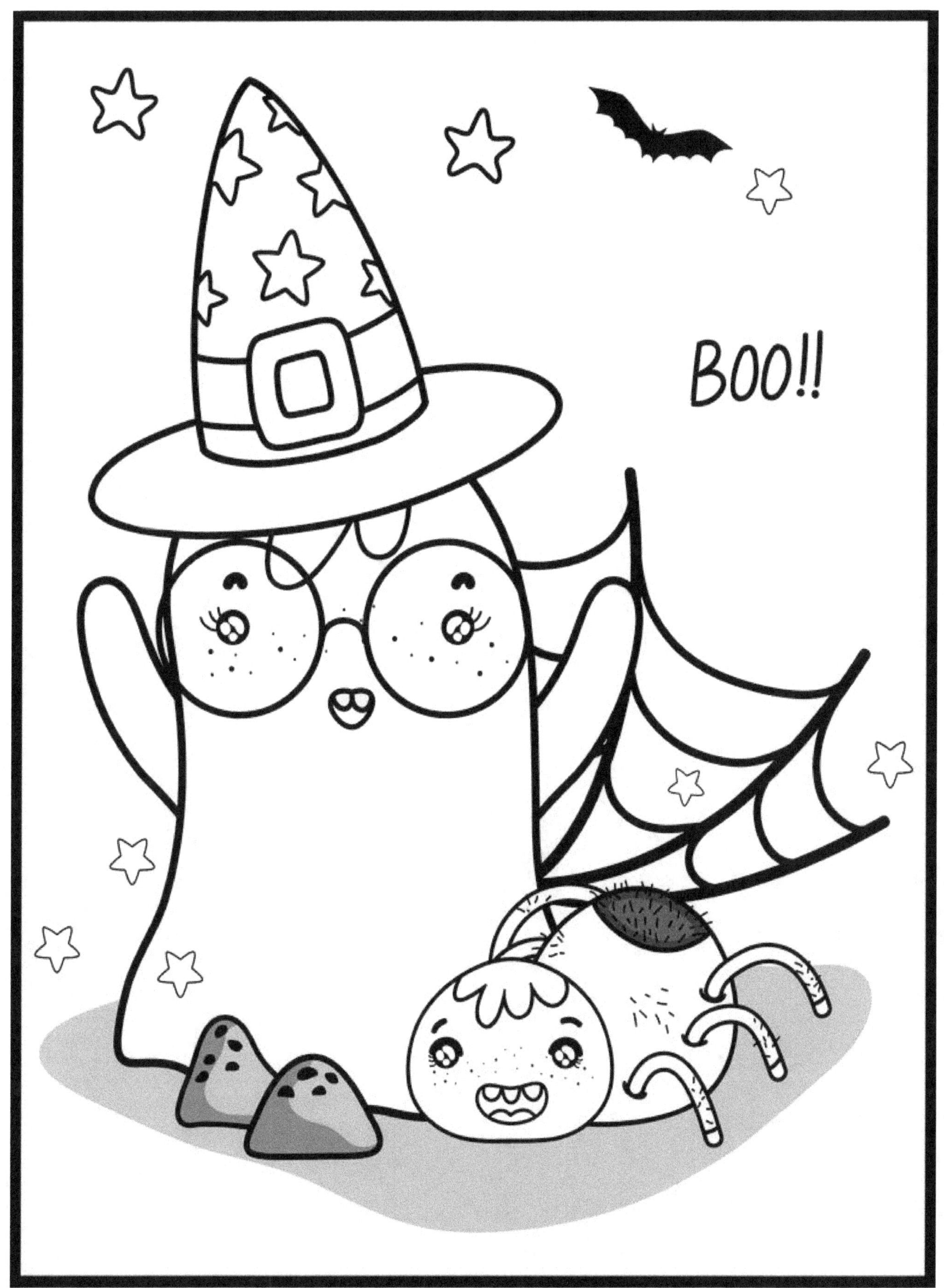
BOO!!

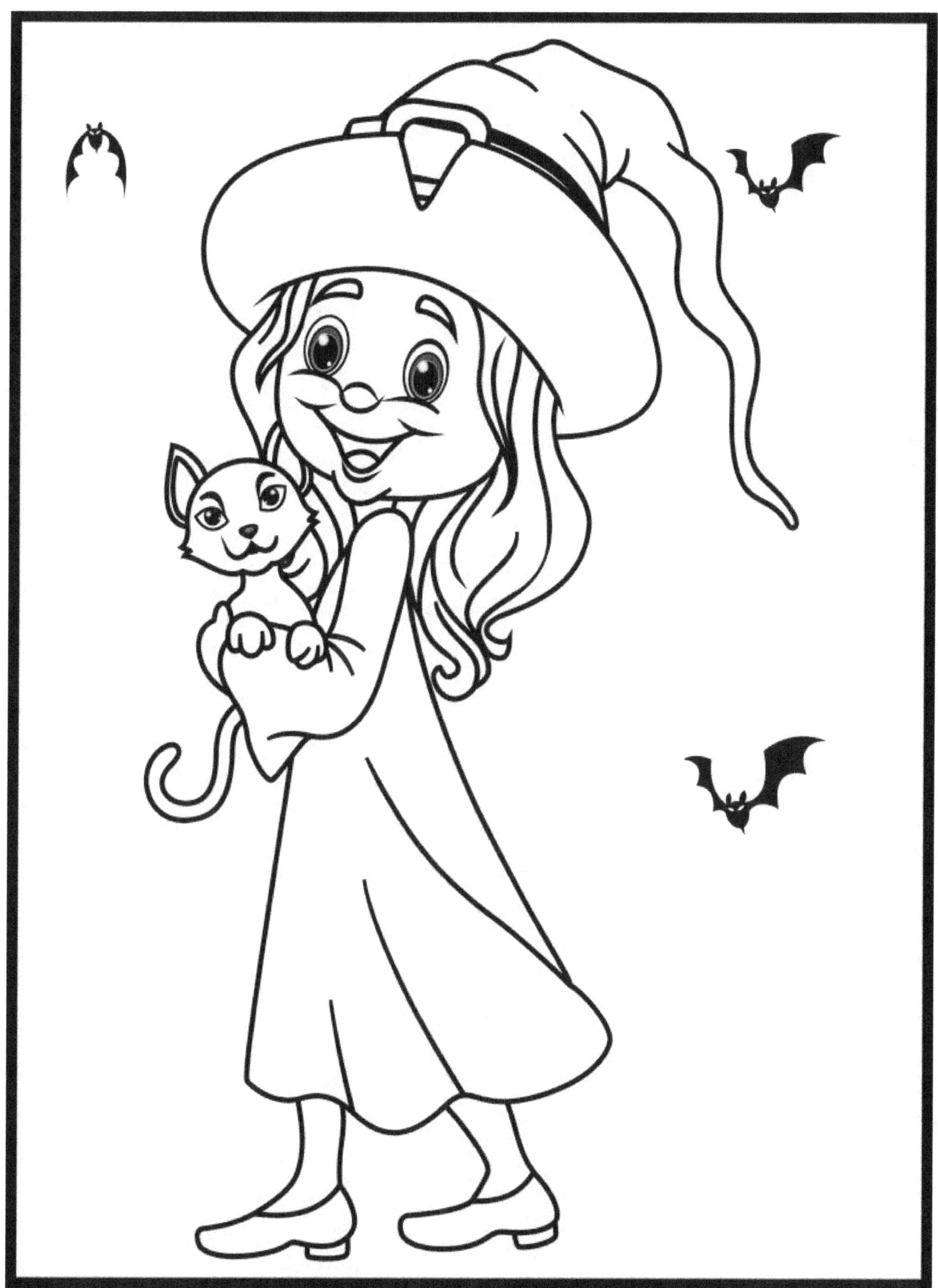

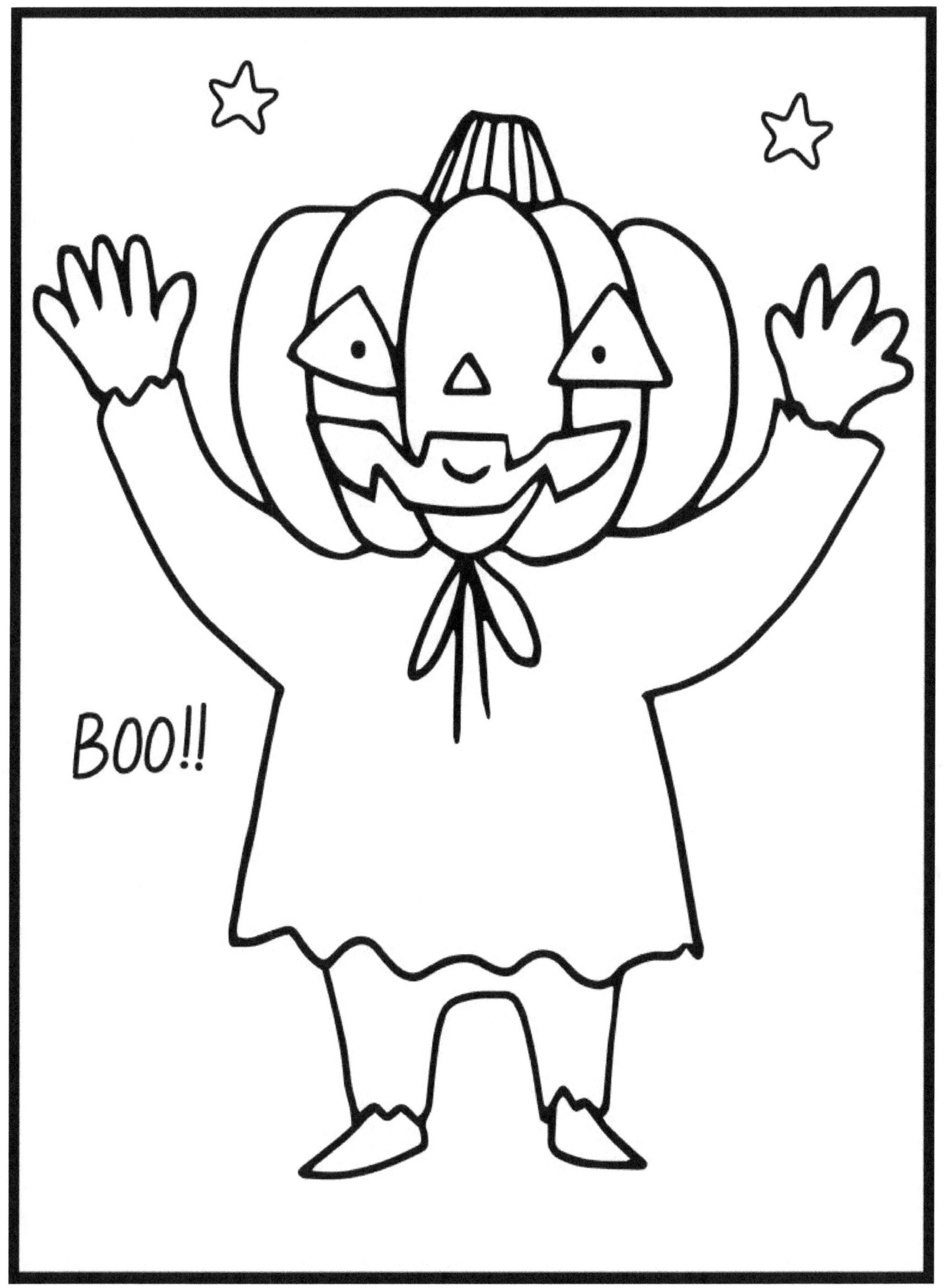
BOO!!

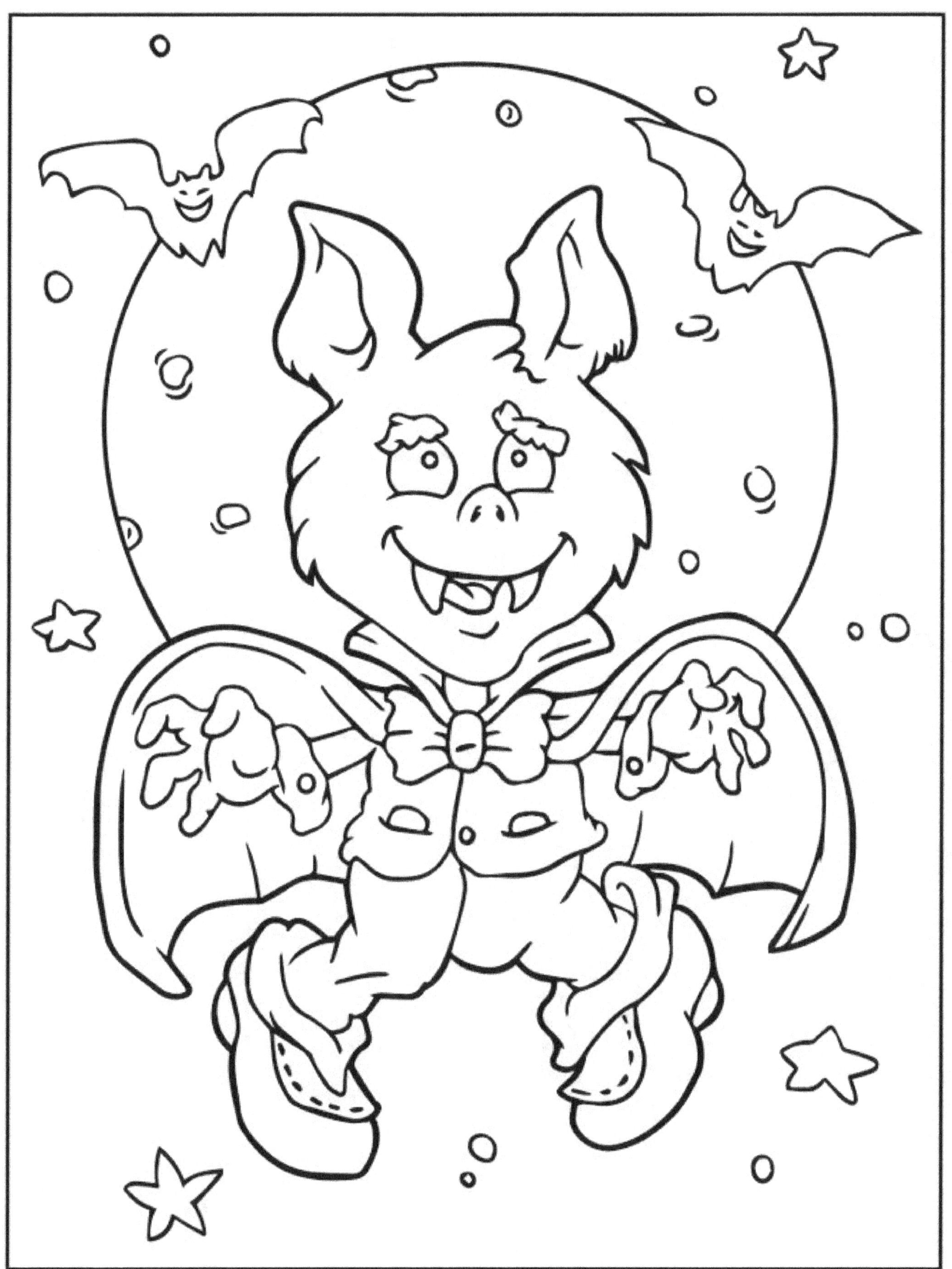

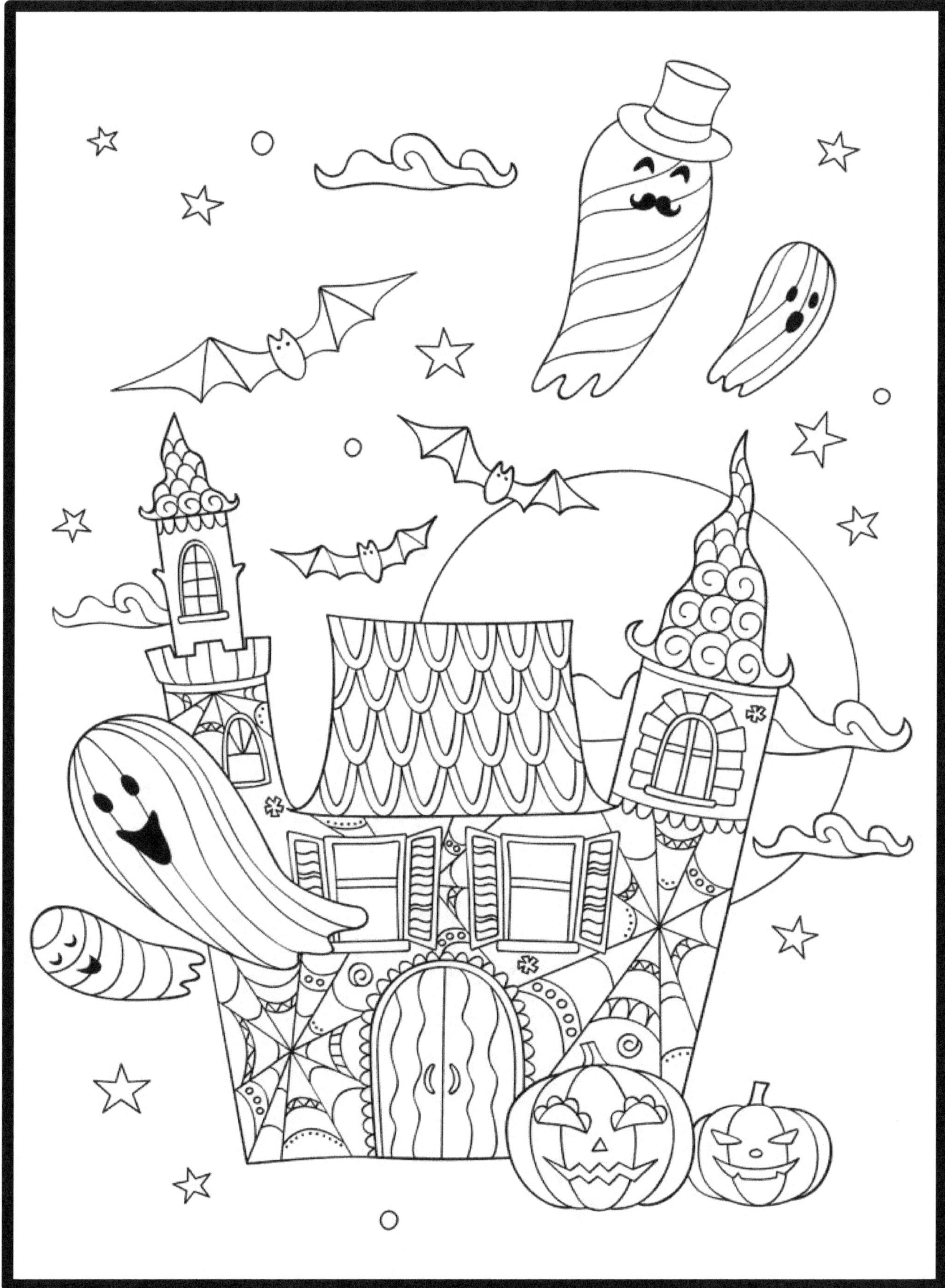

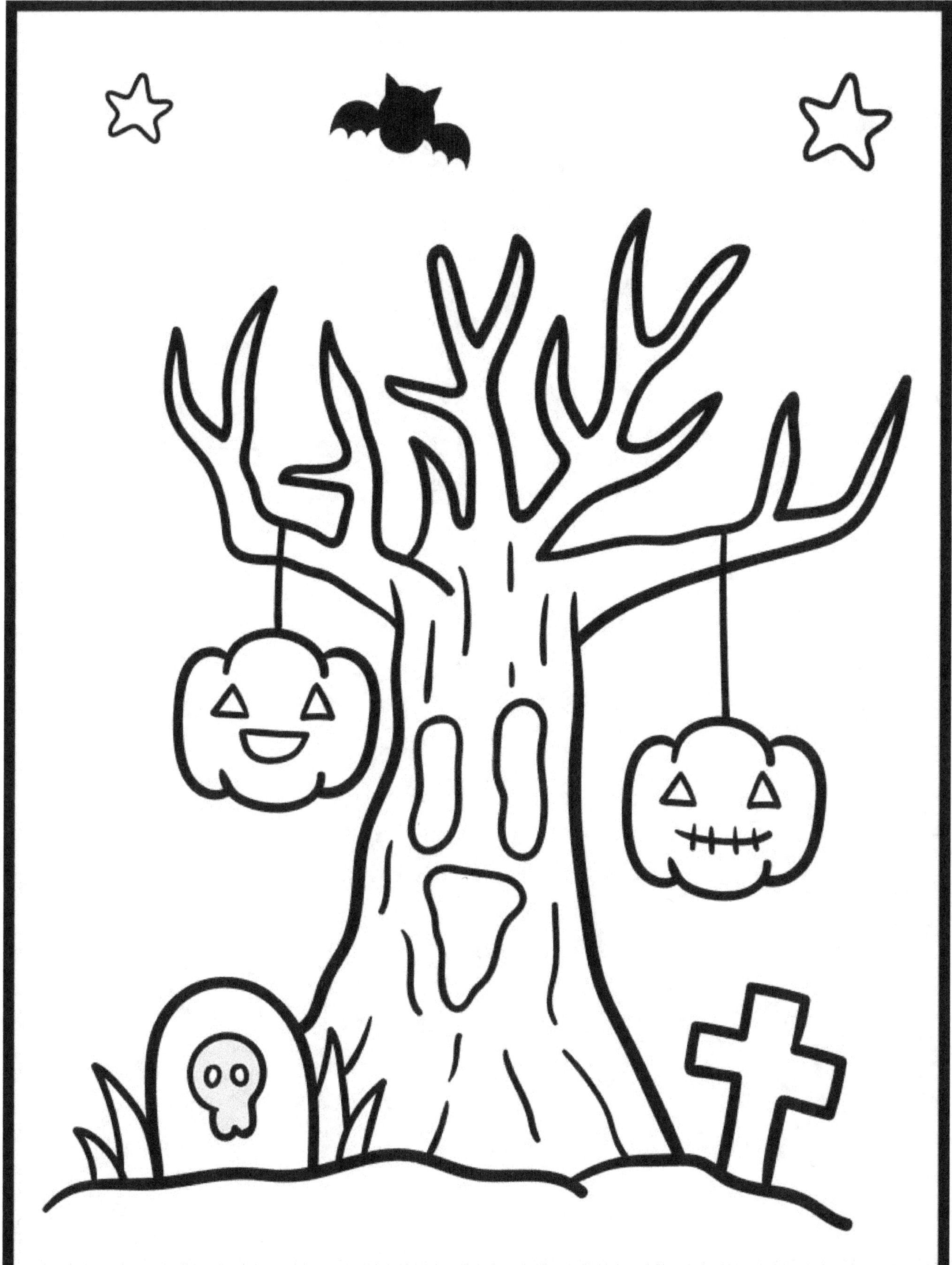

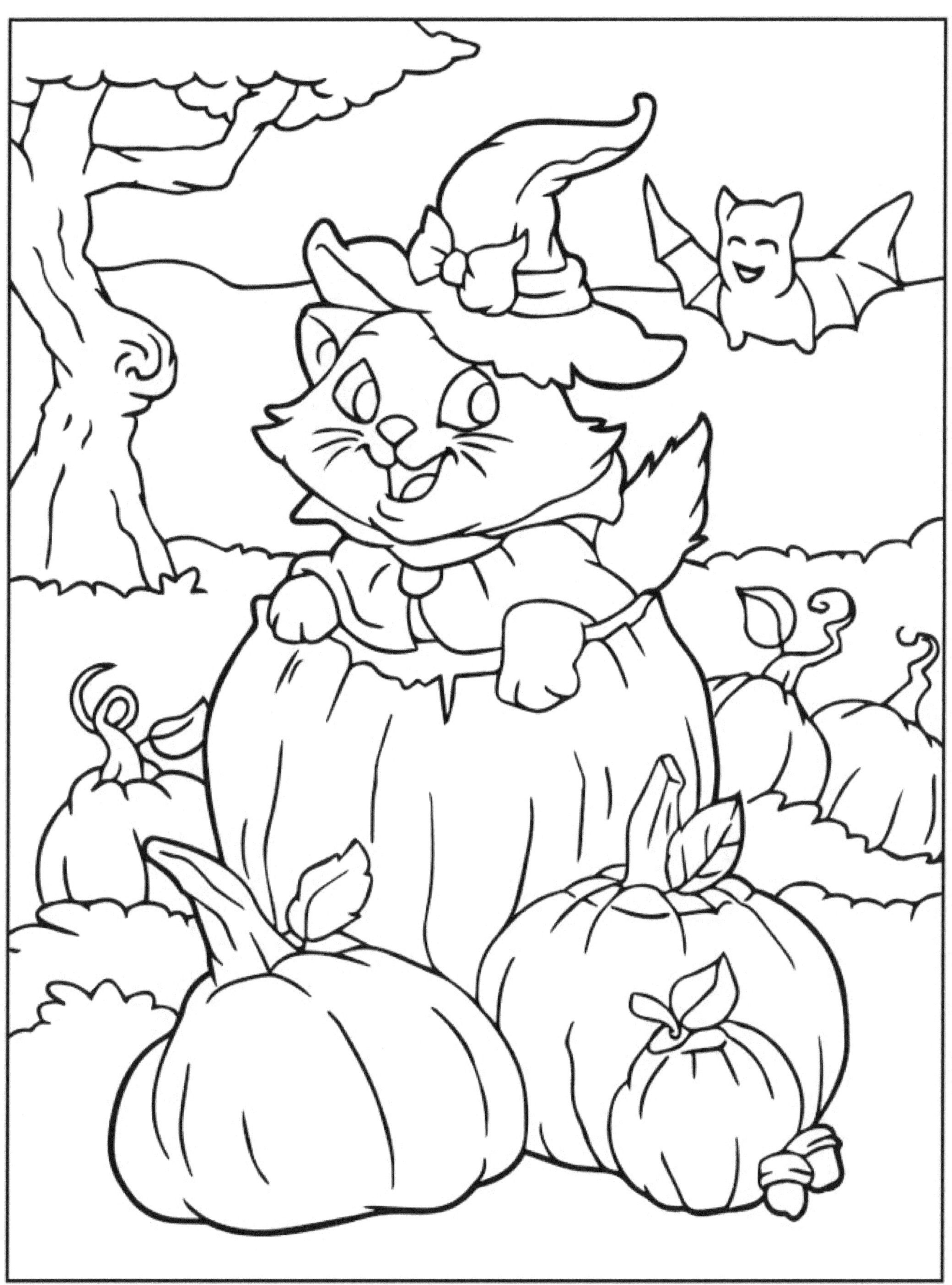

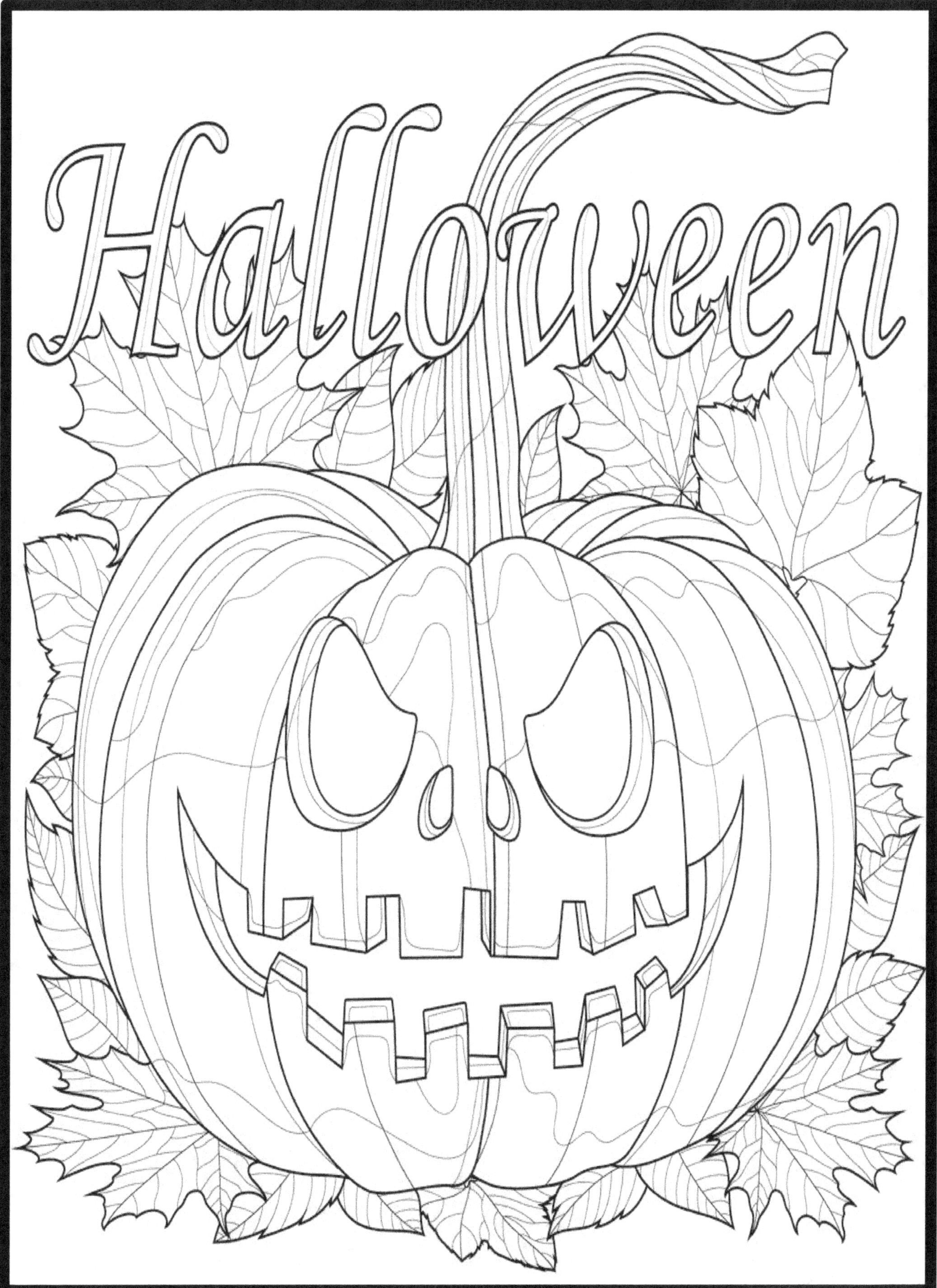
Halloween

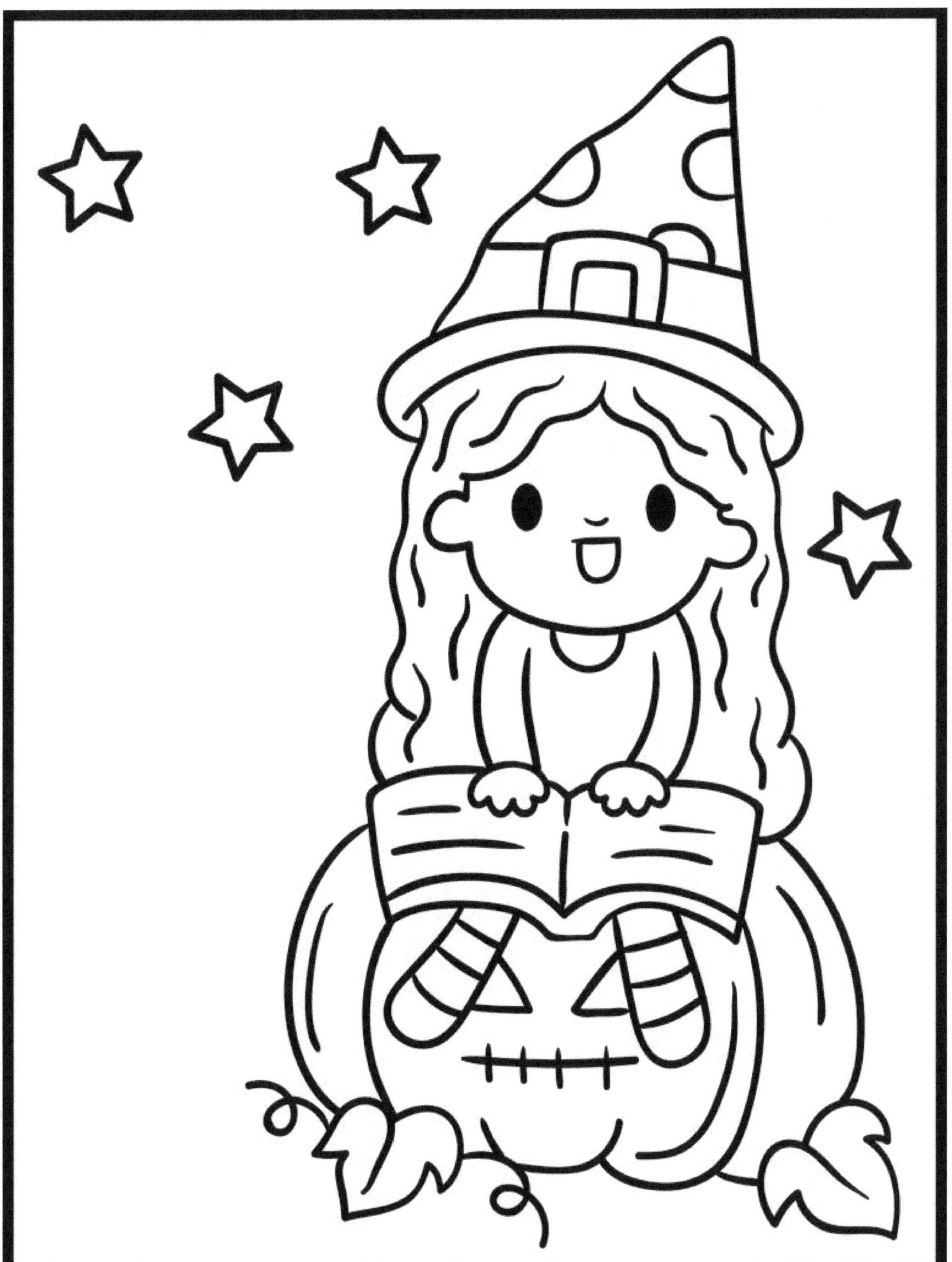

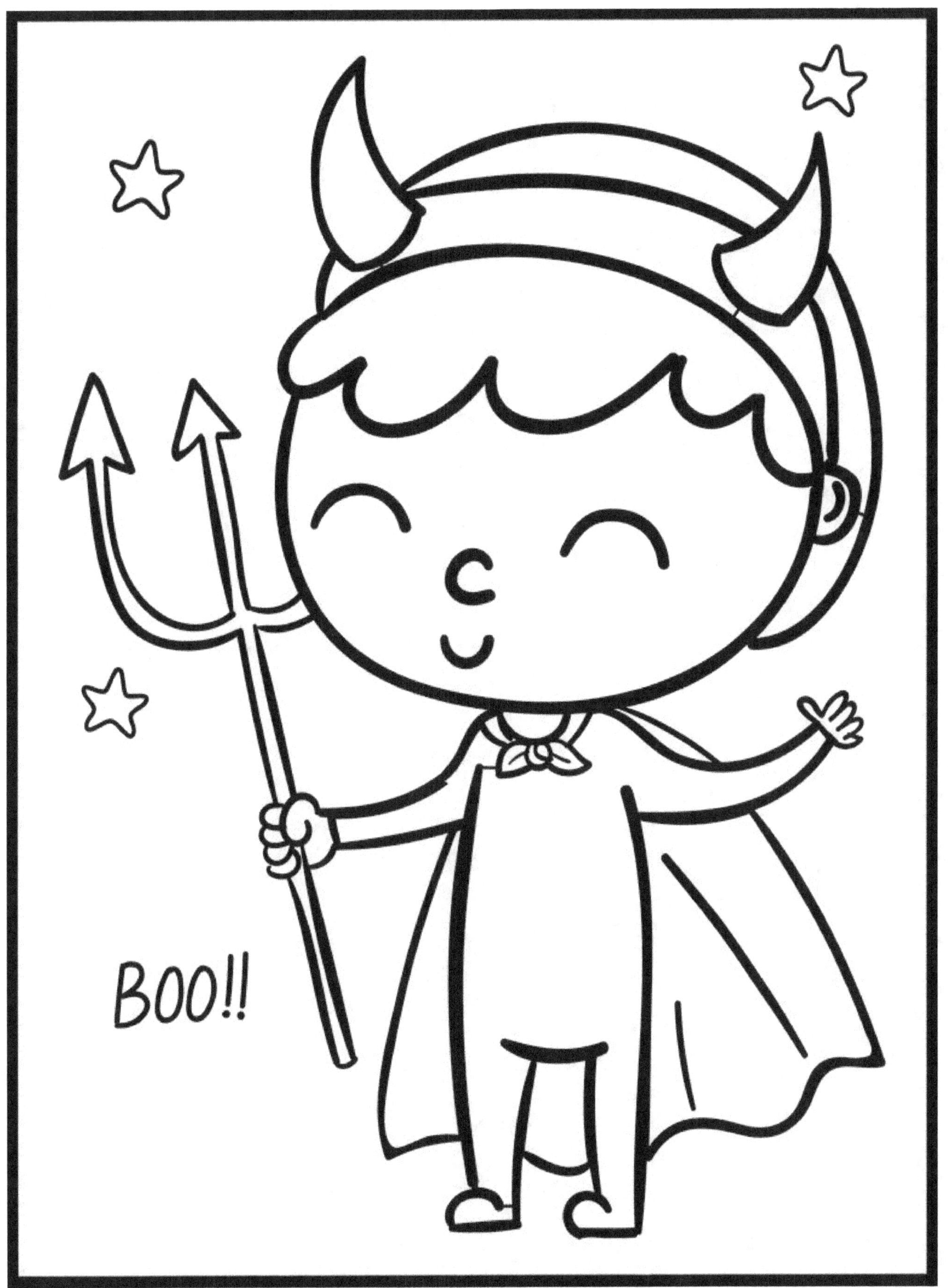
BOO!!